Contents

SPICY ROASTED CHICKPEAS

Time To Prepare: ten minutes

Time to Cook: forty minutes

Yield: Servings 6

INGREDIENTS:

- ¼ teaspoon of cayenne pepper
- 1 teaspoon of paprika
- 1 teaspoon of turmeric
- 2 (fifteen ounce) cans of chickpeas, drained and washed
- 2 teaspoons of coconut oil, melted

DIRECTIONS:

1. Set the oven to 425°F.
2. Coat a baking sheet using a paper towels, then put the chickpeas on them and use more paper towels to take off the surplus water in the chickpeas. Remove all of the paper towels.
3. Place the oil and spices to the chickpeas and mix thoroughly.
4. Roast your chickpeas for forty minutes, stirring every ten minutes.
5. Once the chickpeas are done, take it off from the oven and let fully cool.

NUTRITIONAL INFO: Total Carbohydrates: 19g ,Fiber: 6g ,Net Carbohydrates: ,Protein: 7g ,Total Fat: 4g Calories: 138

ALMOND BLUEBERRY SMOOTHIE

Time To Prepare: ten minutes

Time to Cook: 0 minutes

Yield: Servings 1

INGREDIENTS:

- 1 banana
- 1 cup frozen blueberries
- 1 tbsp. almond butter
- 1/2 cup almond milk
- Water, as required

DIRECTIONS:

1. Put in everything to a blender jug.
2. Cover the jug firmly.
3. Blend until the desired smoothness is achieved. Serve and enjoy!

NUTRITIONAL INFO: Calories: 211 ,Fat: 0.2 g ,Protein: 5.6 g ,Carbohydrates: 3.4 g ,Fiber: 2.3 g

BLACKBERRY ITALIAN DRINK

Time To Prepare: five minutes

Time to Cook: fifteen minutes

Yield: Servings 4

INGREDIENTS:

- 1 bottle sparkling water
- 1 cup blackberries
- 1 lemon, cut
- 2 tbsp. honey

DIRECTIONS:

1. Put in 1 cup (non-carbonated) water to the instant pot.
2. Put in blackberries to the instant pot.
3. Secure the lid. Cook on high pressure ten minutes.
4. When done, depressurize naturally.
5. Mash the berries in the instant pot. Move to dish. Let cool.
6. As blackberries cook, in a separate small deep cooking pan with a heavy bottom. Put in honey. Simmer five minutes. Cool down.
7. To make the drink. Ladle 1 teaspoon honey. Pour in fruit mixture. Put in carbonated water. Stir.

NUTRITIONAL INFO: Calories: 249 ,Fat: 0.6g ,Carbohydrates: 55g ,Protein: 7.5g

BLUEBERRY AND SPINACH SHAKE

Time To Prepare: five minutes

Time to Cook: 0 minutes

Yield: Servings 2

INGREDIENTS:

- 1 cup of low-fat Greek yogurt (not necessary)
- 1 cup of organic blueberries (or washed if non-organic)
- 1/2 cup of spinach
- ice cubes to the desired concentration

DIRECTIONS:

1. Put in ingredients together in a blender until the desired smoothness is achieved and then serve in a tall glass.
2. Drizzle a few fresh berries on top if you prefer!

NUTRITIONAL INFO: Calories: 233 kcal ,Protein: 10.68 g ,Fat: 5.38 g ,Carbohydrates: 37.13 g

ONION, KALE AND WHITE BEAN SOUP

Time To Prepare: fifteen minutes

Time to Cook: twenty-five minutes

Yield: Servings 4

INGREDIENTS:

- ⅛ Teaspoon red pepper flakes (not necessary)
- ¼ cup extra-virgin olive oil
- ¼ teaspoon freshly ground black pepper
- 1 (fifteen½-ounce) can white beans, drained and washed
- 1 big onion, thinly cut
- 1 teaspoon finely chopped fresh rosemary
- 1 teaspoon salt
- 2 garlic cloves, thinly cut
- 3 cups stemmed kale leaves cut into ½-inch pieces
- 4 cups vegetable broth

DIRECTIONS:

1. In a large pot, heat the oil on high heat.
2. Lower the heat to moderate, and put in the onion, garlic, salt, pepper, and red pepper flakes (if using). Sauté until the onion is golden, approximately ten minutes.
3. Put in the kale, and sauté until wilted, one to two minutes.
4. Pour the broth then bring to its boiling point.
5. Lower the heat to simmer, and cook until the kale is tender about five minutes.
6. Put in the beans and rosemary. Cook until the beans are warmed through minimum two to three minutes before you serve.

NUTRITIONAL INFO: Calories: 285 ,Total Fat: 15g ,Total Carbohydrates: 28g ,Sugar: 3g ,Fiber: 9g ,Protein: 13g ,Sodium: 1368mg

PORK STEW

Time To Prepare: five minutes

Time to Cook: 8 hours

Yield: Servings 6

INGREDIENTS:

- 1 onion, finely chopped
- 1 teaspoon dried mixed spices (homemade or store-bought)
- 2 pounds (907 g) pork loin, cut into cubes
- 2 tablespoons olive oil
- 3 cups chicken stock
- 4 garlic cloves, crushed
- From the cupboard:
- Salt and freshly ground black pepper, to taste

DIRECTIONS:

1. Grease the insert of the slow cooker with olive oil.
2. Combine the pork, chicken stock, onion, dried mixed spices, garlic, salt, and black pepper in the slow cooker.
3. Place the slow cooker lid on and cook on low for eight hours.
4. Ladle the stew in a big container and serve warm.

NUTRITIONAL INFO: calories: 381 ,total fat: 18.3g ,carbs: 9.2g ,protein: 42.3g

PUMPKIN AND SAUSAGE SOUP

Time To Prepare: five minutes

Time to Cook: 33 minutes

Yield: Servings 4

INGREDIENTS:

- ½ cup heavy whipping cream
- ½ cup pumpkin puree
- ½ teaspoon dried sage
- ½ teaspoon ground dried thyme
- ½ teaspoon red chili pepper flakes (not necessary)
- 1 garlic clove, minced
- 1 moderate-sized red onion, minced
- 1 pinch salt
- 1 small red bell pepper, diced
- 2 cups chicken broth
- 2 tablespoons butter, melted
- pounds (680 g) fresh sausage

DIRECTIONS:

1. Sauté the sausage in a nonstick frying pan on moderate to high heat for a minutes, then put in the onion and bell pepper. Continue sautéing for about six minutes until the sausage is mildly browned and the onion is translucent.
2. Fold in the chili pepper flakes, thyme, sage, minced garlic, and salt, then put in the pumpkin puree, chicken broth, and heavy whipping cream.
3. Reduce the heat and bring them to a simmer using low heat for fifteen minutes or until it becomes thick.
4. Pour the cooked soup into a big serving container and put in the butter. Stir to mix thoroughly before you serve.

NUTRITIONAL INFO: calories: 777 ,total fat: 70g ,net carbs: 7g ,fiber: 2g ,protein: 27g

PUMPKIN, COCONUT & SAGE SOUP

Time To Prepare: fifteen minutes

Time to Cook: thirty minutes

Yield: Servings 6

INGREDIENTS:

- 1 cup canned pumpkin
- 1 cup full-fat coconut milk
- 1 teaspoon freshly chopped sage
- 2 cloves garlic, chopped
- 6 cups vegetable broth
- Pinch of salt & pepper, to taste

DIRECTIONS:

1. Put in all the ingredients minus the coconut milk to a stockpot on moderate heat and bring to its boiling point. Reduce to a simmer and cook for half an hour
2. Put in the coconut milk and stir.

NUTRITIONAL INFO: Calories: 146 ,Carbohydrates: 7g ,Fiber: 2g Net ,Carbohydrates: 5g ,Fat: 11g ,Protein: 6g

BLUEBERRY LIME JUICE

Time To Prepare: five minutes

Time to Cook: five minutes

Yield: Servings 4

INGREDIENTS:

- 1 cup fresh blueberries
- Water to cover contents
- Zest and juice of 1 lime

DIRECTIONS:

1. Put ingredients in a mesh steamer basket for instant pot. Put in pot.
2. Pour in water to immerse contents.
3. Secure the lid. Cook on high pressure five minutes.
4. When done, depressurize swiftly.
5. Remove steamer basket. Discard cooked produce.
6. Let flavored water cool. Chill completely before you serve.

NUTRITIONAL INFO: Calories: 86 ,Fat: 0g ,Carbohydrates: 22g ,Protein: 0g

BLUEBERRY MATCHA SMOOTHIE

Time To Prepare: five minutes

Time to Cook: 0 minutes

Yield: Servings 2

INGREDIENTS:

- ¼ Teaspoon Ground Cinnamon
- ¼ Teaspoon Ground Ginger
- 1 Banana
- 1 Tablespoon Chia Seeds
- 1 Tablespoon Matcha Powder
- 2 Cups Almond Milk
- 2 Cups Blueberries, Frozen
- 2 Tablespoons Protein Powder, Optional
- A Pinch Sea Salt

DIRECTIONS:

1. Blend all ingredients until the desired smoothness is achieved.

NUTRITIONAL INFO: Calories: 208 ,Protein: 8.7 Grams ,Fat: 5.7 Grams ,Carbohydrates: 31 Grams

BLUEBERRY POMEGRANATE SMOOTHIE

Time To Prepare: five minutes

Time to Cook: 0 minutes

Yield: Servings 2

INGREDIENTS:

- ¼ cup of canned coconut milk
- 1 cup of pomegranate juice, unsweetened
- 1 tbsp. of hemp seeds
- 2 cup of frozen blueberries
- 6 to 8 ice cubes

DIRECTIONS:

1. Mix the smoothie ingredients in your high-speed blender.
2. Pulse the ingredients a few times to cut them up.
3. Combine the mixture on the highest speed setting for thirty to 60 seconds.
4. Pour into glasses and serve.

NUTRITIONAL INFO: Calories: 282 kcal ,Protein: 5.64 g ,Fat: 13.8 g ,Carbohydrates: 37.75 g

BLUEBERRY SMOOTHIE

Time To Prepare: ten minutes

Time to Cook: 0 minutes

Yield: Servings 1

INGREDIENTS:

- 1 banana, peeled
- 1 tbsp. almond butter
- 1 tsp. maca powder
- 1/2 cup almond milk, unsweetened
- 1/2 cup blueberries
- 1/2 cup water
- 1/4 tsp. ground cinnamon
- 2 handfuls baby spinach

DIRECTIONS:

1. In your blender, combine the spinach with the banana, blueberries, almond butter, cinnamon, maca powder, water, and milk.
2. Pulse thoroughly, pour into a glass, before you serve. Enjoy!

NUTRITIONAL INFO: Calories: 341 ,Fat: 12 g ,Protein: 10 g ,Carbohydrates: 54 g ,Fiber: 12 g

BROCCOLI SMOOTHIE

Time To Prepare: five minutes

Time to Cook: 0 minutes

Yield: Servings 4

INGREDIENTS:

- 1 ½ cups strawberries
- 1 ½ cups water
- 1 cup broccoli florets
- 1 cup chopped spinach
- 2 bananas, cut, frozen
- 2 cups frozen mango chunks
- 2 cups pineapple juice

DIRECTIONS:

1. Combine all ingredients into a blender and blend until the desired smoothness is achieved.
2. Pour into 4 tall glasses before you serve.

NUTRITIONAL INFO: Calories: 222 kcal ,Protein: 3.51 g ,Fat: 1.98 g ,Carbohydrates: 51.45 g

CARROT AND ORANGE TURMERIC DRINK

Time To Prepare: five minutes

Time to Cook: 0 minutes

Yield: Servings 2

INGREDIENTS:

- 1 cup orange juice

- 1 tbsp. lemon juice
- 1/2 inch ginger slice
- 1/4 tsp. turmeric powder
- 2 carrots, peeled, chopped
- 2 tbsp. sugar

DIRECTIONS:
1. In a blender, put in orange juice, sugar, turmeric powder, carrots, and lemon juice.
2. Blend well.
3. Serve!

NUTRITIONAL INFO: Calories: 153 kcal ,Protein: 4.47 g ,Fat: 3.3 g ,Carbohydrates: 27.02 g

CHERRY SMOOTHIE

Time To Prepare: five minutes

Time to Cook: 0 minutes

Yield: Servings 4-6

INGREDIENTS:
- 1 ½ cups vanilla Greek yogurt
- 2 bananas, cut
- 3 cups cherry juice
- 3 cups pitted, froze dark sweet cherries
- Fresh cherries, pitted
- Mint sprigs
- To decorate: Optional

DIRECTIONS:
1. Combine all ingredients into a blender and blend until the desired smoothness is achieved.
2. Pour into 4 tall glasses.
3. Decorate using optional ingredients if using before you serve.

NUTRITIONAL INFO: Calories: 114 kcal ,Protein: 2.36 g ,Fat: 1.88 g ,Carbohydrates: 23.49 g

CHOCOLATE CHERRY SMOOTHIE

Time To Prepare: five minutes

Time to Cook: 0 minutes

Yield: Servings 2

INGREDIENTS:
- 2 cups almond milk, unsweetened
- 2 dates, pitted, chopped or 2 teaspoons pure maple syrup

- 2 scoops protein powder or 4 tablespoons almond butter (not necessary)
- 4 cups pitted, frozen cherries
- 4 tablespoons cocoa or cacao powder
- Cacao nibs
- Granola
- Hemp hearts
- To serve: Optional

DIRECTIONS:

1. Combine all ingredients into a blender and blend until the desired smoothness is achieved.
2. Pour into 2 tall glasses and serve topped with optional ingredients.

NUTRITIONAL INFO: Calories: 339 kcal ,Protein: 16.37 g ,Fat: 21.34 g ,Carbohydrates: 27.99 g

ALMOND BUTTER SMOOTHIES

Time To Prepare: five minutes

Time to Cook: 0 minutes

Yield: Servings 1

INGREDIENTS:

- 1 banana, if possible frozen for a creamier shake
- 1 cup of hemp milk
- 1 scoop of hemp protein
- 1 Tablespoon natural almond butter
- few ice cubes

DIRECTIONS:

1. Blend all ingredients together and enjoy!

NUTRITIONAL INFO: Calories: 533 kcal ,Protein: 31.23 g ,Fat: 26.31 g ,Carbohydrates: 47.13 g

APPLE CINNAMON WATER

Time To Prepare: five minutes

Time to Cook: five minutes

Yield: Servings 4

INGREDIENTS:

- 1 whole apple, diced
- 5 cinnamon sticks
- Water to cover contents

DIRECTIONS:

1. Put ingredients in the steamer basket. Put in pot.

2. Put in water cover contents.
3. Secure the lid. Cook on high pressure five minutes.
4. When done, depressurize swiftly.
5. Remove steamer basket. Discard cooked produce.
6. Let flavored water cool. Chill completely before you serve.

NUTRITIONAL INFO: Calories: 194 ,Fat: 0g ,Carbohydrates: 12g ,Protein: 0g

BABY KALE PINEAPPLE SMOOTHIE

Time To Prepare: five minutes

Time to Cook: 0 minutes

Yield: Servings 1

INGREDIENTS:

- 1 cup almond milk
- 1 cup Kale
- 1 tablespoon hemp protein powder
- 1/2 cup frozen pineapple

DIRECTIONS:

1. Put the almond milk, pineapple, and greens in the blender and blend until the desired smoothness is achieved.

NUTRITIONAL INFO: Calories: 389 kcal ,Protein: 20.29 g ,Fat: 16.2 g ,Carbohydrates: 42.29 g

BEET AND CHERRY SMOOTHIE

Time To Prepare: five minutes

Time to Cook: 0 minutes

Yield: Servings 4

INGREDIENTS:

- ½ cup frozen cherries, pitted
- ½ teaspoon frozen banana
- 1 tablespoon almond butter
- 10-ounce almond milk, unsweetened
- 2 small beets, peeled and slice into four

DIRECTIONS:

1. Put in all ingredients in a blender.
2. Blend until the desired smoothness is achieved.

NUTRITIONAL INFO: Calories 470 ,Carbohydrates: 24 g ,Fat: 38 g ,Protein: 16 g

HIBISCUS TEA

Time To Prepare: five minutes

Time to Cook: ten minutes

Yield: Servings 4

INGREDIENTS:

- 1 tbsp. honey
- 1 tsp fresh ginger, grated
- 10 cups water
- 2 cup dried hibiscus petals
- Rind from 1 pineapple

DIRECTIONS:

1. Wash hibiscus leaves meticulously with cold water.
2. Take away the dust.
3. Put in water, honey, and ginger to the instant pot. Stir.
4. Mix in hibiscus petals and pineapple rind.
5. Secure the lid. Cook on HIGH pressure ten minutes.
6. When done, depressurize naturally.
7. Remove pineapple rind. Pass liquid through a fine-mesh strainer.
8. Cool thoroughly. Chill before you serve.

NUTRITIONAL INFO: Calories: 114 ,Fat: 0g ,Carbohydrates: 28g ,Protein: 0g

HOT APPLE CIDER

Time To Prepare: five minutes

Time to Cook: fifteen minutes

Yield: Servings 4

INGREDIENTS:

- ½ cup fresh cranberries
- ½ cup honey
- ½ star of anise
- ½ tsp whole cloves
- 1 lemon, peeled, cut into segments
- 1 orange, peeled, cut into segments
- 2 cinnamon sticks
- 7 medium apples, cored, quarter
- Water to cover ingredients

DIRECTIONS:

1. Put in apples, lemon, orange, and cranberries to the instant pot.

2. Put in cinnamon stick, star anise, and cloves.
3. Pour in water to immerse ingredients.
4. Secure the lid. Cook on HIGH pressure fifteen minutes.
5. Depressurize naturally.
6. Mash fruit using a masher to release juices.
7. Strain the liquid. Chill completely before you serve.

NUTRITIONAL INFO: Calories: 153 ,Fat: 9g ,Carbohydrates: 14g ,Protein: 4g

HOT PEPPERMINT VANILLA LATTE

Time To Prepare: five minutes

Time to Cook: five minutes

Yield: Servings 4

INGREDIENTS:

- ¼ cup honey
- 1 tsp vanilla
- 2 cups coffee
- 23 drops peppermint oil
- 4 cups almond milk

DIRECTIONS:
1. Put in listed ingredients to the instant pot.
2. Secure the lid. Cook on high pressure five minutes.
3. When done, depressurize naturally.
4. Serve warm.

NUTRITIONAL INFO: Calories: 279 ,Fat: 3g ,Carbohydrates: 61g ,Protein: 3g

INSTANT HORCHATA

Time To Prepare: five minutes

Time to Cook: five minutes

Yield: Servings 4

INGREDIENTS:

- 1 cinnamon stick, broken into little chunks
- 32 ounces rice milk
- 6 tbsp. honey

DIRECTIONS:
1. Put in listed ingredients to the instant pot.
2. Secure the lid. Cook on high pressure five minutes.
3. When done, depressurize naturally over ten minutes.

4. Cool thoroughly. Chill before you serve.

NUTRITIONAL INFO: Calories: 226 ,Fat: 1g ,Carbohydrates: 53g ,Protein: 2g

JAMAICAN HIBISCUS TEA

Time To Prepare: five minutes

Time to Cook: five minutes

Yield: Servings 4

INGREDIENTS:

- ½ tsp ginger, minced
- 1 cup dried hibiscus flowers
- 1 tbsp. honey
- 8 cups water
- Ice as required
- Juice of 1 lime

DIRECTIONS:

1. Put in hibiscus flowers, water, honey, and ginger to the instant pot.
2. Secure the lid. Cook on high pressure five minutes.
3. When done, depressurize naturally.
4. Cool thoroughly. Move to glass decanter. Mix in lime Juice. Pour over ice.

NUTRITIONAL INFO: Calories: 197 ,Fat: 0g ,Carbohydrates: 18g ,Protein: 0g

KALE SMOOTHIE

Time To Prepare: ten minutes

Time to Cook: 0 minutes

Yield: Servings 2

INGREDIENTS:

- 10 kale leaves
- 2 pears, chopped
- 5 bananas, peeled and slice into chunks
- 5 cups almond milk
- 5 tbsp. almond butter

DIRECTIONS:

1. In your blender, combine the kale with the bananas, pears, almond butter, and almond milk.
2. Pulse thoroughly, split into glasses, before you serve. Enjoy!

NUTRITIONAL INFO: Calories: 267 ,Fat: 11 g ,Protein: 7 g ,Carbohydrates: fifteen g ,Fiber: 7 g

BEET SMOOTHIE

Time To Prepare: ten minutes

Time to Cook: 0 minutes

Yield: Servings 2

INGREDIENTS:
- 1 tbsp. almond butter
- 1/2 banana, peeled and frozen
- 1/2 cup cherries, pitted
- 10 oz. almond milk, unsweetened
- 2 beets, peeled and quartered

DIRECTIONS:
1. In your blender, combine the milk with the beets, banana, cherries, and butter.
2. Pulse thoroughly, pour into glasses, before you serve. Enjoy!

NUTRITIONAL INFO: Calories: 165 ,Fat: 5 g ,Protein: 5 g ,Carbohydrates: 22 g ,Fiber: 6 g

BERRY SHRUB

Time To Prepare: ten minutes

Time to Cook: twenty minutes

Yield: Servings 4

INGREDIENTS:
- ½ a cup of chopped fresh oregano
- 1 cup of dried elderberries
- 2 cups of apple cider vinegar
- 2 cups of honey
- 2 cups of water

DIRECTIONS:
1. Put in listed ingredients to the instant pot.
2. Secure the lid. Cook on high pressure twenty minutes.
3. When done, depressurize naturally.
4. Pour ingredients through a sieve into a jar.
5. Let cool down. Chill.

NUTRITIONAL INFO: Calories: 127 ,Fat: 0g ,Carbohydrates: 6g ,Protein: 0g

BLACKBERRY & GINGER MILKSHAKE

Time To Prepare: five minutes

Time to Cook: 0 minutes

Yield: Servings 2

INGREDIENTS:

- 1 thumb-sized piece of ginger, grated
- 2 cups of almond milk
- 2 cups of blackberries, washed
- 2 cups of chopped peaches

DIRECTIONS:

1. Combine all ingredients to a blender or juicer and blend until the desired smoothness is achieved.
2. Serve with a scattering of fresh blackberries and enjoy!

NUTRITIONAL INFO: Calories: 619 kcal ,Protein: fifteen.42 g ,Fat: 11.63 g ,Carbohydrates: 123.04 g

CHOCOLATE LATTE WITH REISHI

Time To Prepare: five minutes

Time to Cook: ten minutes

Yield: Servings 2

INGREDIENTS:

- 1 teaspoon Reishi powder
- 2 tablespoons coconut butter
- 4 cups almond milk, unsweetened
- 4 teaspoons raw cacao powder
- A pinch ground cinnamon
- A pinch sea salt
- Sweetener of your choice

DIRECTIONS:

1. Put in almond milk into a deep cooking pan. Put the deep cooking pan using low heat.
2. When the milk is warm and just starts to bubble, remove the heat. Move into a blender.
3. Put in the remaining ingredients and blend for 30 – 40 seconds or until the desired smoothness is achieved.
4. Pour into mugs before you serve.

NUTRITIONAL INFO: Calories: 461 kcal ,Protein: 19.32 g ,Fat: 30.57 g ,Carbohydrates: 28.08 g

BLENDED COCONUT MILK AND BANANA BREAKFAST SMOOTHIE

Time To Prepare: ten minutes

Time to Cook: 0 minutes

Yield: Servings 4

INGREDIENTS:

- 2 cups almond milk
- 2 cups coconut milk
- 4 ripe moderate-sized bananas
- 4 tbsp. flax seeds
- 4 tsp. cinnamon

DIRECTIONS:

1. Peel the banana and cut it into ½-inch pieces. Put all the ingredients in the blender and blend into a smoothie.
2. Put in a dash of cinnamon at the top of the smoothie before you serve.

NUTRITIONAL INFO: Calories: 332 kcal ,Protein: 12.49 g ,Fat: 14.42 g ,Carbohydrates: 42.46 g

COOKED ICED TEA

Time To Prepare: two minutes

Time to Cook: 4 minutes

Yield: Servings 4

INGREDIENTS:

- 2 tbsp. honey
- 4 regular tea bags
- 6 cups water

DIRECTIONS:

1. Put in ingredients to the instant pot.
2. Secure the lid. Cook on high pressure 4 minutes.
3. When done, depressurize naturally.
4. Allow to cool to room temperature. Serve over ice.

NUTRITIONAL INFO: Calories: 22 ,Fat: 0g ,Carbohydrates: 6g ,Protein: 0g

CUCUMBER KIWI GREEN SMOOTHIE

Time To Prepare: five minutes

Time to Cook: 0 minutes

Yield: Servings 2

INGREDIENTS:

- ¼ cup of canned coconut milk
- 1 cup of coconut water
- 1 cup of seedless cucumber, chopped

- 2 ripe kiwi fruit
- 2 tbsps. of fresh chopped cilantro
- 6 to 8 ice cubes
- ice cubes

DIRECTIONS:

1. Mix the smoothie ingredients in your high-speed blender.
2. Pulse the ingredients a few times to cut them up.
3. Combine the mixture on the highest speed setting for thirty to 60 seconds.
4. Pour into glasses and serve.

NUTRITIONAL INFO: Calories: 140 kcal ,Protein: 5.1 g ,Fat: 10.52 g ,Carbohydrates: 7.4 g

CUCUMBER MELON SMOOTHIE

Time To Prepare: five minutes

Time to Cook: 0 minutes

Yield: Servings 2

INGREDIENTS:

- 1 ½ cups of chopped honeydew
- 1 cup of chilled coconut water
- 1 cup of seedless cucumber, diced
- 2 tbsp. of fresh mint
- 6 to 8 ice cubes

DIRECTIONS:

1. Mix the smoothie ingredients in your high-speed blender.
2. Pulse the ingredients a few times to cut them up.
3. Combine the mixture on the highest speed setting for thirty to 60 seconds.
4. Pour into glasses and serve.

NUTRITIONAL INFO: Calories: 300 kcal ,Protein: 5.83 g ,Fat: 8.55 g ,Carbohydrates: 51.21 g

DREAMY YUMMY ORANGE CREAM SMOOTHIE

Time To Prepare: five minutes

Time to Cook: 0 minutes

Yield: Servings 2

INGREDIENTS:

- ¼ cup of fresh orange juice
- ½ cup of canned full-fat coconut milk

- 1 cup of almond milk
- 1 navel orange, peel removed
- 6 to 8 ice cubes

DIRECTIONS:

1. Mix the smoothie ingredients in your high-speed blender.
2. Pulse the ingredients a few times to cut them up.
3. Combine the mixture on the highest speed setting for thirty to 60 seconds.
4. Pour into glasses and serve.

NUTRITIONAL INFO: Calories: 269 kcal ,Protein: 8.63 g ,Fat: 21.36 g ,Carbohydrates: 12.75 g

FIG SMOOTHIE

Time To Prepare: five minutes

Time to Cook: 0 minutes

Yield: Servings 2

INGREDIENTS:

- 1 Banana
- 1 Cup Almond Milk
- 1 Cup Whole Milk Yogurt, Plain
- 1 Tablespoon Almond Butter
- 1 Teaspoon Flaxseed, Ground
- 1 Teaspoon Honey, Raw
- 3-4 Ice Cubes
- 7 Figs, Halved (Fresh or Frozen)

DIRECTIONS:

1. Blend all together ingredients until the desired smoothness is achieved, and serve instantly.

NUTRITIONAL INFO: Calories: 362 ,Protein: 9 Grams ,Fat: 12 Grams ,Carbohydrates: 60 Grams

FLU FIGHTING TONIC

Time To Prepare: five minutes

Time to Cook: ten minutes

Yield: Servings 2

INGREDIENTS:

- ½ teaspoon turmeric powder
- 2 tablespoons clear honey if possible manuka
- Boiling water, as required
- Juice of 2 lemons

- Lemon slices to decorate

DIRECTIONS:

1. Split the lemon juice into 2 mugs. Put in ¼ teaspoon turmeric powder into each mug.
2. Put in a tablespoon of honey into each mug.
3. Pour boiling water to fill up the mugs. Stir.
4. Decorate using a slice of lemon before you serve.

NUTRITIONAL INFO: Calories: 123 kcal ,Protein: 3.59 g ,Fat: 3.23 g ,Carbohydrates: 22.78 g

FRESH CRANBERRY AND LIME JUICE

Time To Prepare: five minutes

Time to Cook: 0 minutes

Yield: Servings 2

INGREDIENTS:

- 1/2½ cups of mixed berries (frozen are fine)
- 1/2½ cups of spinach
- 2 limes, juiced
- 4 cups of cranberries

DIRECTIONS:

1. Mix all the ingredients with water in a juicer until pureed and serve instantly over ice.

NUTRITIONAL INFO: Calories: 578 kcal ,Protein: 6.83 g ,Fat: 9.92 g ,Carbohydrates: 119.35 g

FRESH TROPICAL JUICE

Time To Prepare: five minutes

Time to Cook: 0 minutes

Yield: Servings 2

INGREDIENTS:

- 1 whole pineapple, peeled and slice into chunks.
- 1 cup of water
- 1/2 can of low-fat coconut milk

DIRECTIONS:

1. Put in all ingredients to a juicer and blend until the desired smoothness is achieved.
2. Serve over ice.

NUTRITIONAL INFO: Calories: 116 kcal ,Protein: 3.72 g ,Fat: 3.13 g ,Carbohydrates: 19.55 g

GINGER ALE

Time To Prepare: five minutes

Time to Cook: thirty minutes

Yield: Servings 4

INGREDIENTS:

- 1 pound fresh ginger, unpeeled, diced
- 1 quart carbonated water
- 1 tbsp. honey
- Ice for serving
- Juice and rind of 2 lemons
- Lime wedges

DIRECTIONS:

1. Put ginger and lemon juice in a food processor. Pulse to smooth consistency.
2. Move puree to the instant pot. Mix in honey.
3. Put in lemon peel to the instant pot.
4. Secure the lid. Cook on high pressure thirty minutes.
5. When done, depressurize naturally. Strain and chill.
6. Serve over ice.

NUTRITIONAL INFO: Calories: 108 ,Fat: 0g ,Carbohydrates: 28g ,Protein: 0g

GINGER, CARROT, AND TURMERIC SMOOTHIE

Time To Prepare: five minutes

Time to Cook: 0 minutes

Yield: Servings 2

INGREDIENTS:

- ½ cup Mango, fresh or frozen chunks
- 1 big Carrot, peeled and chopped
- 1 cup Coconut water
- 1 Orange, peeled and separated
- 1 tbsp. Hemp seeds, raw, shelled
- 1 tsp. Ginger, ground
- 1 tsp. Turmeric, ground
- 1/8 tsp. Cayenne pepper

DIRECTIONS:

1. Puree all of the ingredients with one-half cup of ice until the desired smoothness is achieved and drink instantly.

NUTRITIONAL INFO: Calories 250 ,35 grams sugar ,4.5 grams fat ,7 grams fiber ,48 grams carbs ,6 grams protein

GOLDEN CHAI LATTE

Time To Prepare: five minutes

Time to Cook: ten minutes

Yield: Servings 2

INGREDIENTS:

- ¼ teaspoon ground cinnamon
- ½ cup water
- ½ tablespoon maple syrup
- ½ tablespoon turmeric powder
- 1 ¼ cups cashew milk or any other non-dairy milk of your choice
- 1 teaspoon loose leaf chai tea
- 1/8 teaspoon ground nutmeg
- A pinch ground cardamom

DIRECTIONS:

1. Put in water and 1-cup milk into a deep cooking pan. Put the deep cooking pan on moderate heat.
2. Put in chai leaves in a tea strainer (the type that that has a lid and you can close). Lower the strainer in the deep cooking pan. Put in spices.
3. When it just comes to a light boil, remove the heat. Allow it to cool for five minutes. Take out the tea strainer and discard the leaves.
4. Put in maple syrup and stir.
5. Pour into glasses. Sprinkle remaining cashew milk on top. Decorate using cinnamon and nutmeg before you serve.

NUTRITIONAL INFO: Calories: 142 kcal ,Protein: 8.59 g ,Fat: 6.26 g ,Carbohydrates: 13.3 g

GREEN VANILLA SMOOTHIE

Time To Prepare: ten minutes

Time to Cook: 0 minutes

Yield: Servings 1

INGREDIENTS:

- 1 1/2 cups fresh spinach leaves
- 1 banana, cut in chunks
- 1 cup grapes
- 1 tub (6 oz.) vanilla yogurt
- 1/2 apple, cored and chopped

DIRECTIONS:

1. Put in everything to a blender jug.
2. Cover the jug firmly.
3. Blend until the desired smoothness is achieved. Serve and enjoy!

NUTRITIONAL INFO: Calories: 131 ,Fat: 0.2 g ,Protein: 2.6 g ,Carbohydrates: 9.1 g ,Fiber: 1.3 g

PINEAPPLE AND GREENS SMOOTHIE

Time To Prepare: five minutes

Time to Cook: 0 minutes

Yield: Servings 2

INGREDIENTS:

- ¾ cup of almond milk
- 1 cup of chopped spinach
- 1 cup of frozen pineapple
- 1 small frozen banana
- 1 tbsp. of honey
- 2 tbsp. Of chia seeds

DIRECTIONS:

1. Mix the smoothie ingredients in your high-speed blender.
2. Pulse the ingredients a few times to cut them up.
3. Combine the mixture on the highest speed setting for thirty to 60 seconds.
4. Pour into glasses and serve.

NUTRITIONAL INFO: Calories: 272 kcal ,Protein: 5.27 g ,Fat: 4.5 g ,Carbohydrates: 56.37 g

PINEAPPLE- GINGER SMOOTHIE

Time To Prepare: five minutes

Time to Cook: 0 minutes

Yield: Servings 1

INGREDIENTS:

- ½ inch thick ginger, cut
- 1 cup coconut milk
- 1 cup pineapple slice

DIRECTIONS:

1. Put all ingredients in a blender.
2. Pulse until the desired smoothness is achieved.
3. Chill before you serve.

NUTRITIONAL INFO: Calories 299 ,Fat: 8 g ,Protein: 9 g ,Carbohydrates: 51 g

PINEAPPLE SMOOTHIE

Time To Prepare: ten minutes

Time to Cook: 0 minutes

Yield: Servings 2

INGREDIENTS:

- 1 1/2 cups pineapple chunks
- 1 cup coconut water
- 1 orange, peeled and slice into quarters
- 1 tbsp. fresh grated ginger
- 1 tsp. chia seeds
- 1 tsp. turmeric powder
- A pinch black pepper

DIRECTIONS:

1. In your blender, combine the coconut water with the orange, pineapple, ginger, chia seeds, turmeric, and black pepper.
2. Pulse thoroughly, pour into a glass.
3. Makes for a great breakfast!

NUTRITIONAL INFO: Calories: 151 ,Fat: 2 g ,Protein: 4 g ,Carbohydrates: 12 g ,Fiber: 6 g

PINK CALIFORNIA SMOOTHIE

Time To Prepare: ten minutes

Time to Cook: 0 minutes

Yield: Servings 1

INGREDIENTS:

- 1 container (8 oz.) lemon yogurt
- 1/3 cup orange juice
- 7 big strawberries

DIRECTIONS:

1. Put in everything to a blender jug.
2. Cover the jug firmly.
3. Blend until the desired smoothness is achieved. Serve and enjoy!

NUTRITIONAL INFO: Calories: 144 ,Fat: 0.4 g ,Protein: 5.6 g ,Carbohydrates: 8 g ,Fiber: 2.3 g

PUMPKIN PIE SMOOTHIE

Time To Prepare: five minutes

Time to Cook: 0 minutes

Yield: Servings 2

INGREDIENTS:

- ½ Cup Pumpkin, Canned & Unsweetened
- 1 Banana
- 1 Cup Almond Milk
- 1 Teaspoon Ground Cinnamon
- 1 Teaspoon Ground Nutmeg
- 1 Teaspoon Maple Syrup, Pure
- 1 Teaspoon Vanilla Extract Pure
- 2 Tablespoons Almond Butter, Heaping
- 2-3 Ice Cubes

DIRECTIONS:

1. Blend all ingredients together until the desired smoothness is achieved.

NUTRITIONAL INFO: Calories: 235 ,Protein: 5.6 Grams ,Fat: 11 Grams ,Carbohydrates: 27.8 Grams

PURPLE FRUIT SMOOTHIE

Time To Prepare: ten minutes

Time to Cook: 0 minutes

Yield: Servings 1

INGREDIENTS:

- 2 frozen bananas, cut in chunks
- 1 cup orange juice
- 1 tbsp. honey, optional
- 1 tsp. vanilla extract, optional
- 1/2 cup frozen blueberries

DIRECTIONS:

1. Put in everything to a blender jug.
2. Cover the jug firmly.
3. Blend until the desired smoothness is achieved. Serve and enjoy!

NUTRITIONAL INFO: Calories: 133 ,Fat: 1.1 g ,Protein: 3.6 g ,Carbohydrates: 7.6 g ,Fiber: 1.3 g

RASPBERRY BANANA SMOOTHIE

Time To Prepare: ten minutes

Time to Cook: 0 minutes

Yield: Servings 1

INGREDIENTS:

- 1 banana
- 1 cup almond milk
- 1 cup frozen raspberries
- 1 cup raspberry yogurt
- 1 tbsp. flaxseed meal
- 1/4 cup Concord grape juice
- 1/4 cup rolled oats
- 16 whole almonds

DIRECTIONS:

1. Put in everything to a blender jug.
2. Cover the jug firmly.
3. Blend until the desired smoothness is achieved and then serve. Enjoy!

NUTRITIONAL INFO: Calories: 214 ,Fat: 0.4 g ,Protein: 5.6 g ,Carbohydrates: 8 g ,Fiber: 2.3 g

RASPBERRY SMOOTHIE

Time To Prepare: ten minutes

Time to Cook: 0 minutes

Yield: Servings 2

INGREDIENTS:

- 1 avocado, pitted and peeled
- 1/2 cup raspberries
- 3/4 cup raspberry juice
- 3/4 cup orange juice

DIRECTIONS:

1. In your blender, combine the avocado with the raspberry juice, orange juice, and raspberries.
2. Pulse thoroughly, split into 2 glasses, before you serve. Enjoy!

NUTRITIONAL INFO: Calories: 125 ,Fat: 11 g ,Protein: 3 g ,Carbohydrates: 9 g ,Fiber: 7 g

SPICY TOMATO SMOOTHIE

Time To Prepare: five minutes

Time to Cook: 0 minutes

Yield: Servings 2

INGREDIENTS:

- ¼ cup chopped red onion
- 1 jalapeño, cut, deseed if you wish
- 1 small bunch cilantro, chopped

- 1 small cucumber
- 2 big carrots, chopped
- 2 cloves garlic, peeled
- 6 small vine tomatoes
- Juice of 2 limes

DIRECTIONS:
1. Combine all ingredients into a blender and blend until the desired smoothness is achieved.
2. Pour into 2 tall glasses before you serve.

NUTRITIONAL INFO: Calories: 269 kcal ,Protein: 24.87 g ,Fat: 8.71 g ,Carbohydrates: 26.89 g

STRAWBERRY OATMEAL SMOOTHIE

Time To Prepare: ten minutes

Time to Cook: 0 minutes

Yield: Servings 1

INGREDIENTS:
- 1 cup soy milk
- 1 banana, broken into chunks
- 14 frozen strawberries
- 1/2 cup rolled oats
- 1/2 tsp. vanilla extract
- 1 1/2 tsp. honey

DIRECTIONS:
1. Put in everything to a blender jug.
2. Cover the jug firmly.
3. Blend until the desired smoothness is achieved. Serve and enjoy!

NUTRITIONAL INFO: Calories: 172 ,Fat: 0.4 g ,Protein: 5.6 g ,Carbohydrates: 8 g ,Fiber: 2 g

SWEET & SAVOURY SMOOTHIE

Time To Prepare: five minutes

Time to Cook: 0 minutes

Yield: Servings 2

INGREDIENTS:
- 1 apple, peeled and cut
- 1 banana, peeled and cut
- 1 cup of almond or soy milk
- 1 cup of fresh pineapple, peeled and cut
- 1 tbsp. of lemon juice

- 1/2 tbsp. of ginger, grated
- 1/4 tsp of ground turmeric
- 2 cups of carrots, peeled and cut
- 2 cups of filtered water.

DIRECTIONS:

1. Blend carrots and water to make a pureed carrot juice.
2. Pour into a Mason jar or sealable container, cover, and store in the refrigerator.
3. When done, put in the rest of the smoothie ingredients to a blender or juicer until the desired smoothness is achieved.
4. Put in the carrot juice in at the end, blending meticulously until the desired smoothness is achieved.
5. Serve with or without ice.

NUTRITIONAL INFO: Calories: 225 kcal ,Protein: 6.03 g ,Fat: 5.78 g ,Carbohydrates: 39.93 g

SWEET CRANBERRY JUICE

Time To Prepare: five minutes

Time to Cook: 8 minutes

Yield: Servings 4

INGREDIENTS:

- ½ cup honey
- 1 cinnamon stick
- 1 gallon filtered water
- 4 cups fresh cranberries
- Juice of 1 lemon

DIRECTIONS:

1. Put in cranberries, ½ of water, cinnamon cling to the instant pot.
2. Secure the lid. Cook on HIGH pressure 8 minutes.
3. Depressurize naturally.
4. Once cool, strain liquid. Put in remaining water.
5. Mix in honey and lemon. Cool thoroughly.
6. Chill before you serve.

NUTRITIONAL INFO: Calories: 184 ,Fat: 0g ,Carbohydrates: 49g ,Protein: 1g

TRIPLE FRUIT SMOOTHIE

Time To Prepare: ten minutes

Time to Cook: 0 minutes

Yield: Servings 1

INGREDIENTS:

- 1 banana, peeled and chopped
- 1 container (8 oz.) peach yogurt
- 1 cup ice cubes
- 1 cup strawberries
- 1 kiwi, cut
- 1/2 cup blueberries
- 1/2 cup orange juice

DIRECTIONS:
1. Put in everything to a blender jug.
2. Cover the jug firmly.
3. Blend until the desired smoothness is achieved. Serve and enjoy!

NUTRITIONAL INFO: Calories: 124 ,Fat: 0.4 g ,Protein: 5.6 g ,Carbohydrates: 8 g ,Fiber: 2.3 g

TROPICAL MANGO COCONUT SMOOTHIE

Time To Prepare: five minutes

Time to Cook: 0 minutes

Yield: Servings 2

INGREDIENTS:
- ½ cup of canned coconut milk
- ½ cup of fresh orange juice
- 1 ½ cups of frozen mango
- 1 ½ tsp of honey
- 1 medium frozen banana
- 1 tbsp. of fresh lemon juice

DIRECTIONS:
1. Mix the smoothie ingredients in your high-speed blender.
2. Pulse the ingredients a few times to cut them up.
3. Combine the mixture on the highest speed setting for thirty to 60 seconds.
4. Pour into glasses and serve.

NUTRITIONAL INFO: Calories: 354 kcal ,Protein: 6.7 g ,Fat: 18.09 g ,Carbohydrates: 47.42 g

TROPICAL PINEAPPLE KIWI SMOOTHIE

Time To Prepare: five minutes

Time to Cook: 0 minutes

Yield: Servings 2

INGREDIENTS:
- 1 ½ cup of frozen pineapple

- 1 cup of canned full-fat coconut milk
- 1 ripe kiwi; peeled and chopped
- 1 tsp of spirulina powder
- 3 tsp of lime juice
- 6 to 8 ice cubes

DIRECTIONS:

1. Mix the smoothie ingredients in your high-speed blender.
2. Pulse the ingredients a few times to cut them up.
3. Combine the mixture on the highest speed setting.
4. Pour into glasses and serve.

NUTRITIONAL INFO: Calories: 480 kcal ,Protein: 7.38 g ,Fat: 31.92 g ,Carbohydrates: 48.35 g

TURMERIC AND GINGER TONIC

Time To Prepare: five minutes

Time to Cook: ten minutes

Yield: Servings 4

INGREDIENTS:

- 1/8 teaspoon cayenne pepper
- 2 tablespoons grated, fresh ginger
- 2 tablespoons grated, fresh turmeric
- 6 cups water
- Juice of 2 lemons
- Maple syrup or honey to taste
- The rind of 2 lemons, peeled

DIRECTIONS:

1. Put in water, ginger, turmeric, cayenne pepper, and lemon rind into a deep cooking pan.
2. Put the deep cooking pan on moderate to high heat. (Do not boil)
3. Once the mixture is hot, remove from heat.
4. Strain into 4 mugs. Put in honey and lemon juice and stir.
5. Serve warm.

NUTRITIONAL INFO: Calories: 48 kcal ,Protein: 2.28 g ,Fat: 1.81 g ,Carbohydrates: 7.03 g

TURMERIC DELIGHT

Time To Prepare: five minutes

Time to Cook: 0 minutes

Yield: Servings 2

INGREDIENTS:

- ¼ Teaspoon Ginger
- ½ Teaspoon Cinnamon
- 1 Banana, Sliced
- 1 Tablespoon Lemon Juice, Fresh
- 1 Teaspoon Turmeric
- 2 Cups Yogurt, Plain & Whole Milk
- 2 Teaspoons Honey, Raw

DIRECTIONS:

1. Combine all ingredients into a blender then blend until the desired smoothness is achieved.

NUTRITIONAL INFO: Calories: 234 ,Protein: 9.3 Grams ,Fat: 8.2 Grams ,Carbohydrates: 33.5 Grams

TURMERIC HOT CHOCOLATE

Time To Prepare: five minutes

Time to Cook: ten minutes

Yield: Servings 2

INGREDIENTS:
- 1/8 tsp. cayenne pepper, optional
- 1/8 tsp. pepper
- 2 cups milk
- 2 tsp. ground turmeric
- 3 tbsp. cacao or cocoa powder
- 4 tsp. coconut oil
- 4 tsp. honey

DIRECTIONS:
1. Put in milk, turmeric, cocoa, and coconut oil into a deep cooking pan. Put the deep cooking pan on moderate heat. Coconut oil and pepper are added because it helps to absorb the turmeric.
2. Whisk regularly until well blended.
3. When it starts to boil, remove from heat. Put in honey, cayenne pepper, and pepper and whisk well.
4. Split into 2 cups before you serve.

NUTRITIONAL INFO: Calories: 339 kcal ,Protein: 12.76 g ,Fat: 21.19 g ,Carbohydrates: 30.35 g

TURMERIC TEA

Time To Prepare: five minutes

Time to Cook: fifteen minutes

Yield: Servings 2

INGREDIENTS:

- ½ teaspoon ground ginger
- ½ teaspoon turmeric powder
- ½ tsp ground cinnamon
- 2 cups water
- 2 lemon juices
- 2 tablespoons honey

DIRECTIONS:

1. Put in water into a deep cooking pan. Put the deep cooking pan on moderate heat.
2. When it starts to boil, put in turmeric, cinnamon, and ginger and stir slowly.
3. Remove the heat. Cover and allow the mixture to steep for 12 – fifteen minutes. Put in honey and lemon juice.
4. Stir and pour into mugs.
5. Serve.

NUTRITIONAL INFO: Calories: 121 kcal ,Protein: 3.57 g ,Fat: 3.2 g ,Carbohydrates: 21.97 g

VANILLA AVOCADO SMOOTHIE

Time To Prepare: ten minutes

Time to Cook: 0 minutes

Yield: Servings 1

INGREDIENTS:

- 1 cup almond milk
- 1 ripe avocado, halved and pitted
- 1/2 cup vanilla yogurt
- 3 tbsp. honey
- 8 ice cubes

DIRECTIONS:

1. Put in everything to a blender jug.
2. Cover the jug firmly.
3. Blend until the desired smoothness is achieved. Serve and enjoy!

NUTRITIONAL INFO: Calories: 143 ,Fat: 1.2 g ,Protein: 4.6 g ,Carbohydrates: 21 g ,Fiber: 2.3 g

VANILLA BLUEBERRY SMOOTHIE

Time To Prepare: five minutes

Time to Cook: 0 minutes

Yield: Servings 1

INGREDIENTS:

- 1 cup fresh blueberries

- 1 tbsp. flaxseed oil
- 2 cups hemp milk
- 2 tbsp. hemp protein powder
- Handful of ice/ 1 cup frozen blueberries

DIRECTIONS:
1. Mix milk and fresh blueberries plus ice (or frozen blueberries) in a blender.
2. Blend for a minute, move to a glass, and mix in flaxseed oil.

NUTRITIONAL INFO: Calories: 1041 kcal ,Protein: 35.21 g ,Fat: 41.04 g ,Carbohydrates: 140.4 g

VANILLA TURMERIC ORANGE JUICE

Time To Prepare: five minutes

Time to Cook: 0 minutes

Yield: Servings 2

INGREDIENTS:
- ½ teaspoon turmeric powder
- 1 teaspoon ground cinnamon
- 2 cups unsweetened almond milk
- 2 teaspoons vanilla extract
- 6 oranges, peeled, separated into segments, deseeded
- Pepper to taste

DIRECTIONS:
1. Juice the oranges. Put in the remaining ingredients.
2. Pour into 2 glasses before you serve.

NUTRITIONAL INFO: Calories: 223 kcal ,Protein: 11.47 g ,Fat: 11.79 g ,Carbohydrates: fifteen.9 g

VOLUPTUOUS VANILLA HOT DRINK

Time To Prepare: ten minutes

Time to Cook: 0 minutes

Yield: Servings 1

INGREDIENTS:
- 1 scoop of hemp protein
- 1/2 Tbsp. ground cinnamon (or more to taste)
- 1/2 Tbsp. vanilla extract
- 3 cups unsweetened almond milk (or 1 1/2 cup full-fat coconut milk + 1 1/2 cups water)
- Stevia to taste

DIRECTIONS:

1. Put the almond milk into a pitcher. Put ground cinnamon, hemp, vanilla extract in a small deep cooking pan on moderate to high heat. Heat until the pure liquid stevia is just melted and then pour the pure liquid stevia mixture into the pitcher.
2. Stir until the pure liquid stevia is well blended with the almond milk. Bring the pitcher in your refrigerator and let it cool for minimum two hours. Stir thoroughly before you serve.

NUTRITIONAL INFO: Calories: 656 kcal ,Protein: 42.12 g ,Fat: 33.05 g ,Carbohydrates: 44.45 g

WASSAIL

Time To Prepare: five minutes

Time to Cook: ten minutes

Yield: Servings 4

INGREDIENTS:

- ½ tsp nutmeg
- 1 inch peeled ginger
- 10 cloves
- 2 vanilla beans, split or 2 Tbsp pure vanilla extract
- 4 cups orange juice
- 5 cinnamon sticks
- 8 cups apple cider
- Zest and juice of 2 lemons

DIRECTIONS:

1. Pour cider and orange juice in the instant pot.
2. Put cinnamon sticks, nutmeg piece, cloves, lemon zest, vanilla beans in the steamer basket.
3. If you didn't use vanilla beans, pour in vanilla extract. Put in lemon juice.
4. Secure the lid. Cook on high pressure ten minutes.
5. When done, depressurize naturally.
6. Discard contents of the steamer basket.
7. Serve hot from the pot.

NUTRITIONAL INFO: Calories: 221 ,Fat: 0g ,Carbohydrates: 42g ,Protein: 0g

WHITE HOT CHOCOLATE

Time To Prepare: five minutes

Time to Cook: six minutes

Yield: Servings 2

INGREDIENTS:

- ¼ cup cocoa powder/butter
- 2 - 2½ Tbsp honey
- 2 tsp vanilla extract
- 3 cups coconut milk
- Pinch of sea salt

DIRECTIONS:

1. Put in milk, cocoa powder/butter, honey, vanilla extract, and salt to the instant pot.
2. Secure the lid. Cook on LOW pressure six minutes.
3. Depressurize swiftly.
4. Use a hand blender to blend contents 25 seconds.
5. Serve hot.

NUTRITIONAL INFO: Calories: 331 ,Fat: 14g ,Carbohydrates: 47g ,Protein: 4g

WONDERFUL WATERMELON DRINK

Time To Prepare: five minutes

Time to Cook: 0 minutes

Yield: Servings 2

INGREDIENTS:

- 1 cup of coconut water
- 1 cup of watermelon chunks
- 1/2 cup of tart cherries
- 2 cups of frozen mixed berries
- 2 tbsp. of chia seeds

DIRECTIONS:

1. Combine all ingredients in a blender or juicer then blend until pureed.
2. Serve instantly and enjoy!

NUTRITIONAL INFO: Calories: 330 kcal ,Protein: 10.22 g ,Fat: 9.71 g ,Carbohydrates: 53.3 g

ZESTY CITRUS SMOOTHIE

Time To Prepare: five minutes

Time to Cook: 0 minutes

Yield: Servings 1

INGREDIENTS:

- 1 cup almond milk
- 1 med orange peeled, cleaned, and cut into sections
- 1 tbsp. flaxseed oil
- 2 tsp hemp protein powder
- half cup lemon juice
- Handful of ice

DIRECTIONS:

1. Mix milk, lemon juice, orange, and ice in a blender.
2. Blend for a minute, move to a glass, and mix in flaxseed oil.

NUTRITIONAL INFO: Calories: 427 kcal ,Protein: 17.5 g ,Fat: 28.88 g ,Carbohydrates: 24.96 g

APPLE AND TOMATO DIPPING SAUCE

Time To Prepare: ten minutes

Time to Cook: 0 minutes

Yield: Servings 2-4

INGREDIENTS:

- ¼ cup of cider vinegar
- ¼ tsp of freshly ground black pepper
- ½ tsp of sea salt
- 1 garlic clove, finely chopped
- 1 large-sized shallot, diced
- 1 tbsp. natural tomato paste
- 1 tbsp. of extra-virgin olive oil
- 1 tbsp. of maple syrup
- 1/8 tsp of ground cloves
- 3 moderate-sized apples, roughly chopped
- 3 moderate-sized tomatoes, roughly chopped

DIRECTIONS:

1. Put oil into a huge deep cooking pan and heat it up on moderate heat.
2. Put in shallot and cook until light brown for approximately 2 minutes.
3. Stir in the tomato paste, garlic, salt, pepper, and cloves for approximately half a minute. Then put in in the apples, tomatoes, vinegar, and maple syrup.
4. Bring to its boiling point then decrease the heat to allow it to simmer for approximately 30 minutes. Allow to cool for twenty additional minutes before placing the mixture into your blender. Combine the mixture until the desired smoothness is achieved.
5. Keep in a mason jar or an airtight container; place in your fridge for maximum 5 days.
6. Serve it on a burger or with fries.

NUTRITIONAL INFO: Calories: 142 kcal ,Protein: 3 g ,Fat: 3.46 g ,Carbohydrates: 26.93 g

BALSAMIC VINAIGRETTE

Time To Prepare: ten minutes

Time to Cook: 0 minutes

Yield: Servings 2-4

INGREDIENTS:

- ¼ tsp of freshly ground black pepper
- ½ cup of extra-virgin olive oil

- ½ cup of rice vinegar
- 1 clove of freshly minced garlic
- 1 tbsp. of honey or maple syrup
- 1 tsp of sea or kosher salt
- 2 tsp of Dijon mustard

DIRECTIONS:
1. Put all ingredients in a mason jar and cover firmly. Shake thoroughly until all ingredients are blended.
2. Keep in your fridge for minimum 30 minutes before you serve to keep its freshness.
3. Serve with a salad or as your meat marinate.

NUTRITIONAL INFO: Calories: 147 kcal ,Protein: 1.85 g ,Fat: 13.21 g ,Carbohydrates: 4.02 g

BEAN POTATO SPREAD

Time To Prepare: twenty-five minutes

Time to Cook: 0 minutes

Yield: Servings 7-8

INGREDIENTS:
- ¼ cup sesame paste
- ½ teaspoon cumin, ground
- 1 cup garbanzo beans, drained and washed
- 1 tablespoon olive oil
- 2 tablespoons lime juice
- 2 tablespoons water
- 4 cups cooked sweet potatoes, peeled and chopped
- 5 garlic cloves, minced
- A pinch of salt

DIRECTIONS:
1. Throw all the ingredients into a blender and blend to make a smooth mix.
2. Move to a container.
3. Serve with carrot, celery, or veggie sticks.

NUTRITIONAL INFO: Calories 156 ,Fat: 3g ,Carbohydrates: 10g ,Fiber: 6g ,Protein: 8g

CASHEW GINGER DIP

Time To Prepare: five minutes

Time to Cook: 0 minutes

Yield: Servings 1

INGREDIENTS:
- ¼ cup filtered water

- ¼ teaspoon salt
- ½ teaspoon ground ginger
- 1 cup cashews, soaked in water for about twenty minutes and drained
- 1 tablespoon extra-virgin olive oil
- 1 teaspoon lemon juice
- 2 garlic cloves
- 2 teaspoons coconut aminos
- Pinch cayenne pepper

DIRECTIONS:

1. In a blender or food processor, put together the cashews, garlic, water, olive oil, aminos, lemon juice, ginger, salt, and cayenne pepper.
2. Put in the mix in a container.
3. Cover and place in your fridge until chilled. You can use store it for 4-5 days in your fridge.

NUTRITIONAL INFO: Calories 124 ,Fat: 9g ,Carbohydrates: 5g ,Fiber: 1g ,Protein: 3g

CREAMY AVOCADO DRESSING

Time To Prepare: ten minutes

Time to Cook: 0 minutes

Yield: Servings 2-4

INGREDIENTS:

- ½ cup of extra-virgin olive oil
- 1 clove of garlic, chopped
- 1 tsp of honey or maple syrup
- 2 small or 1 large-sized avocado, pitted and chopped
- 2 tsp of lemon or lime juice
- 3 tbsp. of chopped parsley
- 3 tbsp. of red wine vinegar
- Onion powder
- Some Kosher salt and ground black pepper

DIRECTIONS:

1. Combine all ingredients into a blender, apart from the oil. As the ingredients are mixed, progressively put in the oil into the mixture. Blend until the desired smoothness is achieved or becomes liquidy.
2. Use as a vegetable or fruit salad dressing. Put in your fridge for maximum 5 days.

NUTRITIONAL INFO: Calories: 300 kcal ,Protein: 4.09 g ,Fat: 27.9 g ,Carbohydrates: 11.41 g

CREAMY HOMEMADE GREEK DRESSING

Time To Prepare: ten minutes

Time to Cook: 0 minutes

Yield: Servings 2-4

INGREDIENTS:

- ¼ cup non-dairy milk (e.g., almond, rice milk)
- ½ cup of high-quality mayonnaise, without preservatives
- ½ tsp dried basil
- ½ tsp dried oregano
- ½ tsp parsley
- ½ tsp thyme
- 1/3 cup of extra-virgin olive oil
- 1/4 cup of white wine vinegar
- 2 cloves of garlic, minced
- 2 tbsp. of lemon or lime juice
- 2 tsp of honey
- A few tablespoons of water
- Some Kosher salt and pepper

DIRECTIONS:

1. Put all together ingredients in a mason jar and shake, cover firmly, and shake thoroughly. Place in your fridge for a few hours before you serve or serve instantly on your favorite vegetable or fruit salad.
2. Shake well before use. Put in your fridge for maximum 5 days.
3. You may put in a few tablespoons of water to tune the consistency as per your preference.

NUTRITIONAL INFO: Calories: 474 kcal ,Protein: 2.08 g ,Fat: 50.1 g ,Carbohydrates: 5.31 g

CREAMY RASPBERRY VINAIGRETTE

Time To Prepare: ten minutes

Time to Cook: 0 minutes

Yield: Servings 2-4

INGREDIENTS:

- ½ cup of raspberries
- 1 tbsp. of Dijon mustard
- 1 tbsp. of Greek yogurt
- 1/3 cup of extra-virgin olive oil
- 2 tbsp. of honey or maple syrup
- 2 tbsp. of raspberry vinegar

DIRECTIONS:

1. Put all together the ingredients apart from the oil into a blender, in accordance with the ordered list. Cover and blend for ten seconds, by slowly increasing the speed.
2. After 10 seconds, reduce the speed and progressively put in the oil into the mixture. Keep the speed at a stable pace until all of the oil has been poured in. Blend until blended.

3. Store in a mason jar then place in your fridge for maximum 5 days. Serve with a vegetable or fruit salad.

NUTRITIONAL INFO: Calories: 151 kcal ,Protein: 2.22 g ,Fat: 9.47 g ,Carbohydrates: 14.65 g

CREAMY SIAMESE DRESSING

Time To Prepare: ten minutes

Time to Cook: 0 minutes

Yield: Servings 2-4

INGREDIENTS:

- ¼ cup of non-dairy milk (e.g., almond, rice, soymilk)
- ¼ cup of unsweetened peanut sauce
- 1 cup of mayonnaise
- 1 tbsp. of honey or maple syrup
- 1 tbsps. freshly chopped cilantro
- 2 tbsp. of unsalted peanuts
- 2 tbsp. rice vinegar

DIRECTIONS:

1. Put all ingredients apart from the cilantro and peanuts into a blender and blend until the desired smoothness is achieved and creamy. Next, put in in the cilantro and peanuts and pulse the blender a few times until completely crushed and well blended. Put in a mason jar and bring it in your fridge.
2. Serve with a garden salad, pasta or as a dipping sauce.

NUTRITIONAL INFO: Calories: 525 kcal ,Protein: 18.14 g ,Fat: 45.55 g ,Carbohydrates: 11.01 g

CUCUMBER AND DILL SAUCE

Time To Prepare: ten minutes

Time to Cook: 0 minutes

Yield: Servings 2-4

INGREDIENTS:

- ¼ cup of lemon juice
- 1 cucumber, peeled and squeezed to remove surplus liquid
- 1 cup of freshly chopped dill
- 1 tsp of sea salt
- 450g of Greek yogurt

DIRECTIONS:

1. In a moderate-sized container, put together the yogurt, cucumber, and dill then stir until well blended. Put in in the lemon juice and salt to taste.
2. Cover and place in your fridge for approximately 1-2 hours before you serve to keep its freshness. Best serve with Mediterranean food, chips, fish, or even bread.

NUTRITIONAL INFO: Calories: 97 kcal ,Protein: 13.49 g ,Fat: 2.1 g ,Carbohydrates: 6.34 g

DAIRY-FREE CREAMY TURMERIC DRESSING

Time To Prepare: ten minutes

Time to Cook: 0 minutes

Yield: Servings 2-4

INGREDIENTS:
- ½ cup of extra-virgin olive oil
- ½ cup of tahini
- 1 tbsp. of turmeric powder
- 2 tbsp. of lemon juice
- 2 tsp of honey
- Some sea salt and pepper

DIRECTIONS:
1. In a container, whisk all ingredients until well blended.
2. Store in a mason jar and place in your fridge for maximum 5 days.

NUTRITIONAL INFO: Calories: 328 kcal ,Protein: 7.3 g ,Fat: 29.36 g ,Carbohydrates: 12.43 g

HERBY RAITA

Time To Prepare: ten minutes

Time to Cook: 0 minutes

Yield: Servings 2-4

INGREDIENTS:
- ¼ cup of freshly chopped mint
- ¼ tsp of freshly ground black pepper
- ½ tsp of sea salt
- 1 cup of Greek yogurt
- 1 large-sized cucumber, shredded
- 1 tsp of lemon juice

DIRECTIONS:
1. Combine the cucumber with ¼ tsp of salt in a sieve and leave to drain for fifteen minutes. Shake to release any surplus liquid and move to a kitchen towel. Squeeze out as much liquid as you can using the paper towel.
2. Put the cucumber into a medium container then mix in the rest of the ingredients until well blended.

3. Put in your fridge for minimum 2 hours to keep its freshness. Best consume with spicy foods as it could relief the spiciness.

NUTRITIONAL INFO: Calories: 69 kcal ,Protein: 4.33 g ,Fat: 3.66 g ,Carbohydrates: 4.93 g

HOMEMADE GINGER DRESSING

Time To Prepare: ten minutes

Time to Cook: 0 minutes

Yield: Servings 2-4

INGREDIENTS:

- ¼ cup of chopped celery
- ¼ cup of honey or maple syrup
- ¼ cup of water
- ½ cup of chopped carrots
- ½ tsp of white pepper
- 1 cup of chopped onion
- 1 cup of extra-virgin olive oil
- 1 tsp of freshly minced garlic
- 1 tsp of kosher salt
- 2 ½ tbsp. of unsalted, gluten-free soy sauce
- 2 tbsp. of ketchup
- 2/3 cup of rice vinegar
- 6 tbsp. of freshly grated ginger

DIRECTIONS:

1. Put the onion, ginger, celery, carrots, and garlic into a blender. Blend until the mixture are fine but still lumpy from the small vegetable chunks.
2. Put in in the vinegar, water, ketchup, soy sauce, honey or maple syrup, lemon juice, salt, and pepper. Pulse until the ingredients are well blended.
3. Slowly put in the oil while blending, until everything is thoroughly combined. The mixture must be runny but still grainy.
4. Serve with a winter salad.

NUTRITIONAL INFO: Calories: 389 kcal ,Protein: 2.71 g ,Fat: 32.08 g ,Carbohydrates: 22.14 g

HOMEMADE LEMON VINAIGRETTE

Time To Prepare: ten minutes

Time to Cook: 0 minutes

Yield: Servings 2-4

INGREDIENTS:

- ¼ tsp of sea salt
- ½ tsp of Dijon mustard, without preservatives
- ½ tsp of lemon zest
- 1 tsp of honey or maple syrup
- 2 tbsp. of freshly squeezed lemon juice
- 3 tbsp. of extra-virgin olive oil
- Freshly ground black pepper

DIRECTIONS:
1. Whisk all together the ingredients apart from olive oil and black pepper in a small container. Then progressively put in 3 tbsp. of olive oil while continuously whisking until well blended. Put in some ground black pepper to taste.
2. Put mason jar and place in your fridge for maximum 3 days.
3. Serve with a garden salads.

NUTRITIONAL INFO: Calories: 68 kcal ,Protein: 1.69 g ,Fat: 6.06 g ,Carbohydrates: 1.71 g

HOMEMADE RANCH

Time To Prepare: ten minutes

Time to Cook: 0 minutes

Yield: Servings 2-4

INGREDIENTS:
- ¼ cup of Greek yogurt
- ¼ tsp Kosher salt
- ½ cup of natural mayonnaise, without preservatives
- ½ tsp of dried dill
- ½ tsp of dried parsley
- ½ tsp of garlic powder
- ½ tsp of onion powder
- ¾ cup of non-dairy milk
- 1/8 tsp Freshly ground black pepper
- 2 tsp of dried chives

DIRECTIONS:
1. Combine all ingredients apart from the milk into a medium container. Mix together until well blended.
2. Put in in the milk and mix thoroughly.
3. Pour in a mason jar or an airtight container. Serve instantly or place in your fridge for maximum 2 hours to keep the freshness. Put in your refrigerator for maximum 5 days.
4. Serve with a garden or fruit salad.

NUTRITIONAL INFO: Calories: 482 kcal ,Protein: 3.55 g ,Fat: 51.98 g ,Carbohydrates: 1.63 g

HONEY BEAN DIP

Time To Prepare: five minutes

Time to Cook: 0 minutes

Yield: Servings 3-4

INGREDIENTS:

- ¼ teaspoon ground cumin
- ¼ teaspoon salt
- 1 (14-ounce) can each of kidney beans and black beans
- 1 tablespoon apple cider vinegar
- 1 teaspoon lime juice
- 2 cherry tomatoes
- 2 garlic cloves
- 2 tablespoons filtered water
- 2 teaspoons raw honey
- Freshly ground black pepper to taste
- Pinch cayenne pepper to taste

DIRECTIONS:

1. In a blender or food processor, put together the beans, garlic, tomatoes, water, vinegar, honey, lime juice, cumin, salt, cayenne pepper, and black pepper.
2. Blend until it becomes smooth. Put in the mix in a container.
3. Cover and place in your fridge to chill. You can place in your fridge for maximum 5 days.

NUTRITIONAL INFO: Calories 158 ,Fat: 1g ,Carbohydrates: 33g ,Fiber: 8g ,Protein: 9g

SOY WITH HONEY AND GINGER GLAZE

Time To Prepare: ten minutes

Time to Cook: 0 minutes

Yield: Servings 2-4

INGREDIENTS:

- ¼ cup of honey
- 1 tbsp. of rice vinegar
- 1 tsp of freshly grated ginger
- 2 tbsp. gluten-free soy sauce

DIRECTIONS:

1. Put all together the ingredients into a small container and whisk well.
2. Serve with a vegetables, chickens, or seafood.
3. Keep the glaze in a mason jar, firmly covered, and place in your fridge for maximum four days.

NUTRITIONAL INFO: Calories: 90 kcal ,Protein: 2.32 g ,Fat: 1.54 g ,Carbohydrates: 17.99 g

STRAWBERRY POPPY SEED DRESSING

Time To Prepare: ten minutes

Time to Cook: 0 minutes

Yield: Servings 2-4

INGREDIENTS:
- ¼ cup of raspberry vinegar
- ¼ tsp of ground ginger
- ¼ tsp of sea salt
- ½ tsp of onion powder
- ½ tsp of poppy seeds
- 1/3 cup of extra-virgin olive oil
- 1/3 cup of honey
- 2 tbsp. of freshly squeezed orange juice

DIRECTIONS:
1. Put all ingredients, apart from the poppy seeds and oil into a blender. Blend until the desired smoothness is achieved and creamy. Next, progressively put the oil into the mixture until blended. Put in in the poppy seeds and stir thoroughly.
2. Put in a mason jar then place in your fridge before you serve. Keep for maximum 3 days.
3. Serve with your garden salads.

NUTRITIONAL INFO: Calories: 167 kcal ,Protein: 1.84 g ,Fat: 9.35 g ,Carbohydrates: 18.89 g

TAHINI DIP

Time To Prepare: ten minutes

Time to Cook: 0 minutes

Yield: Servings 2-4

INGREDIENTS:
- ¼ cup of tahini
- ½ tsp of maple syrup
- 1 small grated or thoroughly minced clove of garlic (this is optional)
- 1 tbsp. of apple cider vinegar
- 1 tbsp. of freshly squeezed lemon juice
- 1 tbsp. of tamari
- 1 tsp of finely grated ginger, or ½ tsp of ground ginger
- 1 tsp of turmeric
- 1/3 cup of water

DIRECTIONS:

1. Blend or whisk all ingredients together. Place the dressing in an airtight container then place in your fridge for approximately 5 days.
2. Enjoy!

NUTRITIONAL INFO: Calories: 120 kcal ,Protein: 4.77 g ,Fat: 9.63 g ,Carbohydrates: 5.12 g

TOMATO AND MUSHROOM SAUCE

Time To Prepare: ten minutes

Time to Cook: 0 minutes

Yield: Servings 2-4

INGREDIENTS:

- ½ cup of water
- 1 moderate-sized leek, chopped
- 2 moderate-sized carrots, chopped
- 2 stalks of celery, chopped
- 2 tsp of dried oregano
- 4 cloves of garlic, crushed
- 450g of button mushrooms, diced
- 5 tbsp. of coconut milk
- 680g of unsalted tomato puree
- Black pepper, seasoning
- Some sea salt, seasoning

DIRECTIONS:

1. In a big frying pan, place a few tablespoons of water and heat on moderate heat. Once it sizzles, put in in the mushrooms and Sautee for approximately five minutes, stir once in a while.
2. Next, put in in the leek, carrots, and celery. Stir thoroughly and cook for approximately five minutes or until the vegetables are soft. Put in more water if required.
3. Mix in the tomato puree with ½ cup of water and dried oregano. Bring to its boiling point and then decrease the heat to allow it to simmer for approximately fifteen minutes.
4. Remove from heat and mix in the garlic, coconut milk, and salt and pepper to taste.
5. Put in an airtight container, then store for maximum four days in your fridge or freeze for maximum 1 month. Serve with a pasta.

NUTRITIONAL INFO: Calories: 467 kcal ,Protein: 16.91 g ,Fat: 3.81 g ,Carbohydrates: 109.68 g

ALMOND AND HONEY HOMEMADE BAR

Time To Prepare: fifteen minutes + thirty minutes refrigerator time

Time to Cook: fifteen minutes

Yield: Servings 8

INGREDIENTS:

- ¼ cup almond butter
- ¼ cup honey
- ¼ cup sugar (or another sweetener to your taste in adjusted amount)
- ¼ cup sunflower seeds
- ½ teaspoon vanilla extract
- 1 cup oats
- 1 cup whole-grain puffed cereal (unsweetened)
- 1 tbsp. flaxseeds
- 1 tbsp. sesame seeds
- 1/3 cup apricots (dried and chopped)
- 1/3 cup currants
- 1/3 cup raisins (chopped)
- 1/8 tsp salt
- A ¼ cup of almonds

DIRECTIONS:

1. Preheat your oven to 350 degrees Fahrenheit.
2. Place a baking paper to an 8-inch pan or coat it with cooking spray/oil.
3. Combine the almonds, oats, and seeds and spread the mixture on a rimmed baking sheet.
4. Bake the mixture until you notice that the oats are mildly toasted (for approximately ten minutes).
5. Move the mixture to a container.
6. Put in cereal, raisins, currants, and apricots to the container.
7. Toss thoroughly to blend.
8. Mix honey, almond butter, vanilla, salt, and sugar in a deep cooking pan.
9. Heat on moderate heat. Stir regularly for 2-5 minutes until you see light bubbles.
10. Once you notice the bubbles, pour the mixture over the dry mixture with apricots and oats you prepared previously.
11. Mix thoroughly using a spatula. There mustn't be any dry spots.
12. Move the new mixture to the previously prepared pan.
13. Push it to the pan to make a firm and flat layer.
14. Place in your refrigerator for half an hour
15. Chop the layer into eight equal bars or squares, to your taste.
16. Consume instantly or place in your refrigerator up to seven days.

NUTRITIONAL INFO: Calories: 213 kcal ,Protein: 6.92 g ,Fat: 9.59 g ,Carbohydrates: 32.33 g

ALMONDS AND BLUEBERRIES YOGURT SNACK

Time To Prepare: ten minutes

Time to Cook: 0 minutes

Yield: Servings 2

INGREDIENTS:

- 1 ½ cups nonfat Greek yogurt
- 1 cup blueberries
- 20 almonds, chopped

DIRECTIONS:

1. Take 2 bowls and put in ¾ cup yogurt into each container.
2. Split the blueberries among the bowls and stir.
3. Drizzle half the almonds in each container before you serve.

NUTRITIONAL INFO: Calories: 223 kcal ,Protein: 6.57 g ,Fat: 9.45 g ,Carbohydrates: 30.82 g

ANTI-INFLAMMATORY KEY LIME PIE

Time To Prepare: twenty minutes + thirty-five minutes refrigerator time

Time to Cook: 0

Yield: Servings 8

INGREDIENTS:

- ½ cup honey
- ½ cup Medjool dates, chopped and pitted
- 1 cup unsweetened shredded coconut
- 1 cup walnuts
- 1 teaspoon lime zest
- 1/4 teaspoon sea salt
- 3 firm avocados
- 3 tablespoons lime juice
- Lime slices
- Pinch of sea salt

DIRECTIONS:

1. Use a food processor to put all together the walnuts, coconut, and the salt, then pulse until crudely ground.
2. Place the dates and pulse until the mixture resembles bread crumbs, trying to stick together.
3. Push the mixture into the edges and bottom of a non-stick greased 9-inch pie pan. Use your fingers or the back of a spoon to press the crust into a uniform layer. Bring the crust into the freezer for minimum fifteen minutes while preparing the filling.
4. Use the food processor again and mix the avocado, honey, lime juice, lime zest, and salt. Process until the desired smoothness is achieved.
5. Pour the filling into the now-chilled piecrust and place it in your fridge for about twenty minutes.
6. Decorate using fresh lime slices and serve cold. Store any left overs in your fridge.

NUTRITIONAL INFO: Calories: 273 kcal ,Protein: 4.19 g ,Fat: 18.4 g ,Carbohydrates: 28.49 g

ANTS ON A LOG

Time To Prepare: five minutes

Time to Cook: 0 minutes

Yield: Servings 2

INGREDIENTS:
- 3 tablespoons of almond butter
- 3 tablespoons of raisins
- 6 celery sticks

DIRECTIONS:
1. Spread half a tablespoon of almond butter on each celery stick.
2. Top with half a tablespoon of raisins on each celery stick.
3. Split the celery sticks between two plates, and enjoy!

NUTRITIONAL INFO: ,Total Carbohydrates: 17g ,Fiber: 2g ,Net Carbohydrates: ,Protein: 4g ,Total Fat: 14g Calories: 201

APPLE CRISP

Time To Prepare: fifteen minutes

Time to Cook: twenty-five minutes

Yield: Servings 6-8

INGREDIENTS:

Topping:
- 1 ½ cups old-fashioned rolled oats
- 1 teaspoon salt
- ½ cup stevia
- 2 teaspoons ground cinnamon
- 1 cup nuts, crudely chopped
- 3 tablespoon melted coconut oil.
- 1/3 cup almond meal
- 2/3 cup shredded, unsweetened coconut
- 1/4 teaspoon ground nutmeg

Apple filling:
- ½ cup stevia
- 1 tablespoon ground cinnamon
- 1 teaspoon vanilla
- 1/4 cup arrowroot flour
- 1/4 teaspoon salt

- 10 tart apples
- 2 tablespoons fresh-squeezed lemon juice
- 3 tablespoons melted coconut oil
- The zest of 1 orange

DIRECTIONS:

1. Set the oven to 350 F then grease a 9 by a 13-inch baking pan with coconut oil.
2. Put together the topping ingredients in a container, then mix and save for later.
3. Combine the filling ingredients (except for the apples) in a second big container.
4. Leave the skins on the apples, if you wish. Core them and slice super slim (1/8 inch thick).
5. Toss the apples in the filling ingredients to coat uniformly. Put the apple mixture in a baking pan and spread the topping over it all, pushing down tightly.
6. Put in your oven with a pan underneath to catch any drips.
7. Bake for about twenty-five minutes or until the topping is brown and juices are bubbling. Apples must be tender.
8. Cool slightly on a rack then serve.

NUTRITIONAL INFO: Calories: 446 kcal ,Protein: 6.15 g ,Fat: 27.39 g ,Carbohydrates: 57.45 g

APPLE SAUCE TREAT

Time To Prepare: ten minutes

Time to Cook: 0 minutes

Yield: Servings 1

INGREDIENTS:

- ½ teaspoon cinnamon
- 1 ½ teaspoons toasted slivered almonds
- 1/4 cup low Fat cottage cheese
- 1/4 cup unsweetened applesauce

DIRECTIONS:

1. Combine the cottage cheese and applesauce in a container, stirring well.
2. Drizzle with cinnamon and mix thoroughly.
3. Drizzle the top with almonds, pick up your spoon, and enjoy.

NUTRITIONAL INFO: Calories: 225 kcal ,Protein: 16.24 g ,Fat: 14.17 g ,Carbohydrates: 8.54 g

AVOCADO AND EGG SANDWICH

Time To Prepare: ten minutes

Time to Cook: 0 minutes

Yield: Servings 2

INGREDIENTS:

- ½ lime juice
- 1 avocado (ripe)
- 1 egg, organic
- 1 scallion
- 2 radishes
- 2 slices of who wheat, seed bread
- A pinch of salt (sea or Himalayan)
- Black pepper – to your taste
- Mixed seeds – to your choice

DIRECTIONS:

1. Peel the avocado.
2. Boil the egg (soft boiled).
3. Chop the radishes to thin slices.
4. Dice the scallion (finely).
5. Mix avocado, salt, and lime juice in a container. Mash the mixture meticulously.
6. Spread the mixture onto the bread.
7. Put in some radish.
8. Put tender boiled eggs on top.
9. Put in some scallion, seeds, and pepper.

NUTRITIONAL INFO: Calories: 342 kcal ,Protein: 12.36 g ,Fat: 22.99 g ,Carbohydrates: 26.54 g

AVOCADO HUMMUS

Time To Prepare: fifteen minutes

Time to Cook: 0 minutes

Yield: Servings 4

INGREDIENTS:

- .25 cup Sunflower seeds
- .25 cup Tahini
- .25 tsp. Pepper
- .5 cup Cilantro
- .5 cup Coconut oil
- .5 Lemon juice
- .5 tsp. Salt
- 1 clove pressed garlic
- 3 Avocados
- 5 tsp. Cumin

DIRECTIONS:

1. Halve the avocados, take off the pits, then spoon out the flesh.
2. Put all together ingredients in a blender and stir until super smooth.

3. Put in water, lemon juice, or oil if you need to loosen the mixture bit.

NUTRITIONAL INFO: Calories: 651 kcal ,Protein: 9.62 g ,Fat: 64.05 g ,Carbohydrates: 19.95 g

AVOCADO WITH TOMATOES AND CUCUMBER

Time To Prepare: ten minutes

Time to Cook: 0 minutes

Yield: Servings 2

INGREDIENTS:

- ¼ cup cilantro
- ¼ cup olives – to your choice
- ½ red onion
- 1 cucumber
- 1 lemon
- 1 Tbsp. turmeric
- 1/8 cup parsley
- 2 avocados
- 4 Roma tomatoes
- Salt and pepper – to your taste

DIRECTIONS:

1. Dice the tomatoes, cucumber, avocado, and olives.
2. Cut the cilantro, parsley, and onion.
3. Put in the above ingredients into a container.
4. Squeeze the lemon juice then put in to the vegetables.
5. Put in olive oil, turmeric, salt, and pepper.
6. Toss thoroughly.
7. Consume instantly after putting in lemon juice and olive oil.
8. If you prefer to consume the salad later, put in the dressing instantly before consuming it.

NUTRITIONAL INFO: Calories: 480 kcal ,Protein: 11.57 g ,Fat: 35.27 g ,Carbohydrates: 39.77 g

BAKED VEGGIE TURMERIC NUGGETS

Time To Prepare: ten minutes

Time to Cook: twenty-five minutes

Yield: Servings 24

INGREDIENTS:

- ¼ tsp. Black pepper powder

- ¼ tsp. Sea salt
- ½ cup Almond meal
- ½ tsp. Turmeric powder
- 1 big Whole egg
- 1 cup Chopped carrots
- 1 tsp. Minced garlic
- 2 cups Broccoli florets
- 2 cups Cauliflower florets

DIRECTIONS:

1. Preheat your oven to 400°F.
2. Get a parchment-lined baking sheet ready.
3. Pour cauliflower, turmeric, broccoli, carrots, black pepper, garlic, and sea salt in the blender and blitz until it's smooth.
4. Pour in the egg and almond meal and stir until it's blended.
5. Pour the paste into a mixing container. Scoop out a small amount onto your hand and make a circular disc. Put this disc on the baking sheet and repeat the pulse until the mixing container is empty.
6. Slide into the oven then bake for minimum fifteen minutes on one before flipping and baking for about ten minutes on the other side.
7. Serve with a side of Paleo ranch sauce.

NUTRITIONAL INFO: Calories: 12 kcal ,Protein: 0.88 g ,Fat: 0.52 g ,Carbohydrates: 1.12 g

BERRY DELIGHT

Time To Prepare: fifteen minutes

Time to Cook: 0 minutes

Yield: Servings 6

INGREDIENTS:

- ¼ cup of raw honey
- 1 cup of fresh organic blackberries
- 1 cup of fresh organic blueberries
- 1 cup of fresh organic raspberries
- 1 tablespoon of cinnamon

DIRECTIONS:

1. Mix all the berries together in a big container, put in in the honey, and slowly stir.
2. Drizzle with the cinnamon.

NUTRITIONAL INFO: ,Total Carbohydrates: 20g ,Fiber: 3g ,Net Carbohydrates: ,Protein: 1g ,Total Fat: 0g Calories: 78

BERRY ENERGY BITES

Time To Prepare: ten minutes

Time to Cook: 0 minutes

Yield: Servings 6

INGREDIENTS:

- ¼ cup of dried blueberries
- ½ - 1 cup of almond milk
- ½ cup of coconut flour
- 1 tablespoon of coconut sugar
- 1 teaspoon of cinnamon

DIRECTIONS:

1. In a huge mixing container, put together the coconut flour, cinnamon, coconut sugar, and blueberries, and mix thoroughly.
2. Put in the almond milk slowly until a firm dough is formed.
3. Form into bite-sized balls and place in your fridge for thirty minutes so they can harden up.
4. Store leftovers in your fridge.

NUTRITIONAL INFO: ,Total Carbohydrates: 18g ,Fiber: 1g ,Net Carbohydrates: ,Protein: 1g ,Total Fat: 1g Calories: 80

BLUEBERRY & CHIA FLAX SEED PUDDING

Time To Prepare: ten minutes

Time to Cook: fifteen minutes

Yield: Servings 4

INGREDIENTS:

- ¼ cup of blueberries
- 2 cups of almond milk
- 3 tablespoons of chia seeds
- 3 tablespoons of ground flaxseed

DIRECTIONS:

1. Warm a pan on moderate heat then put all together of the ingredients apart from the blueberries.
2. Stir all the ingredients until the pudding is thick, this will take around three minutes.
3. Place the pudding into a container then top with blueberries.

NUTRITIONAL INFO: ,Total Carbohydrates: 23g ,Fiber: 12g ,Net Carbohydrates: ,Protein: 7g ,Total Fat: 15g Calories: 243

BOILED OKRA AND SQUASH

Time To Prepare: five minutes

Time to Cook: five minutes

Yield: Servings 1

INGREDIENTS:

- ½ cup of okra, cut in 1" cubes
- ½ cup of squash, cut in 1" cubes
- 1 clove garlic, minced
- 2/3 cup Vegetable stock or fish stock, plain water may be used as well
- Salt to taste

DIRECTIONS:

1. Boil the liquid in high heat.
2. Put in the okra and squash. Bring to its boiling point. Put in the garlic. Reduced the heat and simmer for minimum five minutes or until the squash is soft.
3. Put in salt to taste and serve hot.

NUTRITIONAL INFO: Calories: 117 kcal ,Protein: 8.2 g ,Fat: 6.25 g ,Carbohydrates: 7.82 g

BROWNIES AVOCADO

Time To Prepare: ten minutes

Time to Cook: twenty-five minutes

Yield: Servings 6-8

INGREDIENTS:

- ½ cup almond meal
- 1 ½ teaspoon instant coffee (with or without caffeine, as you wish)
- 2 teaspoons ground cinnamon
- ½ teaspoon salt
- 2 cups nuts or seeds, chopped
- 1 avocado
- 1 apple, cored and chopped, with the skin on
- 1 cup cooked and diced sweet potato
- 4 tablespoons ground chia seeds
- 1 teaspoon vanilla
- ½ cup almond butter
- ½ cup coconut butter, softened
- 1/4 cup coconut oil
- 2 1/4 cup stevia
- 3/4 cup cocoa powder

DIRECTIONS:

1. Set the oven to 350F then line a 9 by 13-inch pan with parchment. Allow it to overlap the sides to make handles for lifting the brownies out when done.
2. In a container, mix the almond meal, cocoa, coffee, cinnamon, salt, and nuts. Whisk and save for later.
3. Bring the remaining ingredients in a food processor and mix until the desired smoothness is achieved. Put in the ingredients in the container and pulse. This combination must be lumpy.
4. Pour into pan and bake for minimum twenty-five minutes.
5. Allow to cool and chill in your fridge for a couple of hours before cutting. The baked product will be a little gooey, so refrigerating it makes the brownies easier to cut. The chilled results will be fairly crumbly.

NUTRITIONAL INFO: Calories: 591 kcal ,Protein: 11.03 g ,Fat: 53.8 g ,Carbohydrates: 26.58 g

BRUSCHETTA

Time To Prepare: 60 minutes

Time to Cook: 0 minutes

Yield: Servings 4

INGREDIENTS:

- ¼ cup of extra virgin olive oil
- ¼ teaspoon of ground black pepper
- 1 red onion, diced
- 1 teaspoon of sea salt
- 2 cloves of garlic, minced
- 2 tablespoons of balsamic vinegar
- 4 medium tomatoes, diced

DIRECTIONS:

1. Put all together the ingredients into a big container, and stir slowly.
2. Place in your fridge for an hour before you serve on gluten-free toast (toast is not included in nutritional information)

NUTRITIONAL INFO: ,Total Carbohydrates: 8g ,Fiber: 2g ,Net Carbohydrates: ,Protein: 1g ,Total Fat: 14g Calories: 156

BRUSSELS SPROUT CHIPS

Time To Prepare: ten minutes

Time to Cook: ten minutes

Yield: Servings 4

INGREDIENTS:

- 2 cups Brussels sprout leaves
- 2 tablespoons ghee
- Kosher salt
- Lemon zest

DIRECTIONS:

1. Set the oven to 350F, then cover two cookie sheets using parchment paper.
2. Place the leaves in a huge container and pour melted ghee over the top, and put in salt.
3. Bake for minimum 8 to ten minutes or until the leaves are crunchy. If they are tender at all, put them back in your oven.
4. While still hot, drizzle the lemon zest over the leaves. Serve warm.

NUTRITIONAL INFO: Calories: 42 kcal ,Protein: 3.13 g ,Fat: 1.68 g ,Carbohydrates: 4.77 g

BUTTERED BANANA CHICKPEA COOKIES

Time To Prepare: ten minutes

Time to Cook: twelve minutes

Yield: Servings 8

INGREDIENTS:

- ¼-tsp cinnamon
- ¼-tsp salt
- ⅓ -cup chocolate chips
- ⅓ -cup coconut sugar
- ½-cup creamy peanut butter
- 1-pc small banana, very ripe
- 1-tsp baking powder
- 2-Tbsps ground flaxseed
- 2-tsp vanilla extract
- fifteen-oz. chickpeas, washed and drained

DIRECTIONS:

1. Preheat the oven to 350F. Grease a baking pan with cooking spray.
2. Mix in all the ingredients apart from the chocolate chips in your blender. Combine the batter for two minutes, or until turning into a smooth consistency.
3. Mix in the chocolate chips. Ladle the batter to make cookies. Put the cookies in the pan, and bake for about twelve minutes.

NUTRITIONAL INFO: Calories: 372 ,Fat: 12.4g ,Protein: 18.6g ,Sodium: 174mg ,Total Carbohydrates: 58.1g ,Fiber: 11.6g ,Net Carbohydrates: 46.5g

CANDIED DATES

Time To Prepare: five minutes

Time to Cook: 0 minutes

Yield: Servings 2

INGREDIENTS:

- 2 tablespoons of dark cocoa nibs
- 2 tablespoons of peanut butter
- 4 pitted Medjool dates

DIRECTIONS:

1. Cut the pitted dates in half, and spread half a tablespoon of peanut butter on each date.
2. Top each date with half a tablespoon of dark cocoa nibs.
3. Split the candied dates between two plates, and enjoy!

NUTRITIONAL INFO: ,Total Carbohydrates: 20g ,Fiber: 3g ,Net Carbohydrates: ,Protein: 5g ,Total Fat: 12g Calories: 187

CARROT STICKS WITH AVOCADO DIP

Time To Prepare: ten minutes

Time to Cook: 0 minutes

Yield: Servings 6

INGREDIENTS:

- ½ cup cilantro, firmly packed
- ½ onion
- 1 big avocado, pitted
- 1 tablespoon of chili-garlic sauce or chili sauce
- 2 tablespoon olive oil
- 6 ounces shelled edamame
- Juice of one lemon
- Salt and pepper

DIRECTIONS:

1. Put the edamame, cilantro, onion, and chili sauce in a blender or food processor. Pulse it to cut and mix the ingredients. Put in the avocado and the lemon juice. Slowly put in the olive oil as you blend. Move to a jar.
2. Scoop 2 spoons and serve with carrot sticks.

NUTRITIONAL INFO: Calories: 154 kcal ,Protein: 5.16 g ,Fat: 11.96 g ,Carbohydrates: 8.44 g

CAULIFLOWER SNACKS

Time To Prepare: ten minutes

Time to Cook: 60 minutes

Yield: Servings 4

INGREDIENTS:

- 1 head of cauliflower
- 1 teaspoon salt

- 4 tablespoons extra virgin olive oil

DIRECTIONS:
1. Set the oven to 425F, then prepare two cookie sheets by lining them using parchment paper.
2. Trim off the cauliflower florets and discard the core. Chop the florets into golf-ball-sized pieces.
3. Put the cauliflower in a container, and pour olive oil over them and drizzle with salt. Mix to coat. Spread in a single layer, not touching.
4. Roast approximately 1 hour flipping the cauliflower three to four times until a golden-brown color is achieved. Serve warm.

NUTRITIONAL INFO: Calories: 91 kcal ,Protein: 2.93 g ,Fat: 7.7 g ,Carbohydrates: 3.29 g

KIWI STRAWBERRY SMOOTHIE

Time To Prepare: ten minutes

Time to Cook: 0 minutes

Yield: Servings 1

INGREDIENTS:
- ¼ cup Chia seed powder
- ½ cup Strawberries, fresh or frozen, chopped
- 1 Banana, diced
- 1 cup Milk, almond or coconut
- 1 Kiwi, peeled and chopped
- 1 tsp. Basil, ground
- 1 tsp. Turmeric, ground

DIRECTIONS:

1. Drink instantly after all the ingredients have been thoroughly combined.

NUTRITIONAL INFO: Calories 250 ,9.9 grams sugar ,1 gram fat ,34 grams carbs ,4.3 grams fiber ,

LEMON GINGER ICED TEA

Time To Prepare: five minutes

Time to Cook: ten minutes

Yield: Servings 2-3

INGREDIENTS:
- ¼ teaspoon turmeric
- 1 tablespoon fresh lemon juice or to taste (not necessary)
- 1 tablespoon maple syrup
- 2 – 3 lemon slices

- 2 inches fresh ginger, peeled, thinly cut or to taste
- 3-4 cups water
- A pinch ground cinnamon

DIRECTIONS:

1. Pour water into a deep cooking pan. Put in ginger, turmeric, lemon slices, and cinnamon. Put the deep cooking pan on moderate heat.
2. Cover and simmer for eight - ten minutes.
3. Strain and pour into a jar. Place the maple syrup, and lemon juice, then stir. Chill for eight – 10 hours.
4. Stir thoroughly. Pour into glasses before you serve.

NUTRITIONAL INFO: Calories: 55 kcal ,Protein: 2.32 g ,Fat: 2.13 g ,Carbohydrates: 7.47 g

MANGO AND GINGER INFUSED WATER

Time To Prepare: five minutes

Time to Cook: five minutes

Yield: Servings 4

INGREDIENTS:

- 1 cup fresh mango, chopped
- 2-inch piece ginger, peeled, cubed
- Water to cover ingredients

DIRECTIONS:

1. Put ingredients in the mesh steamer basket.
2. Put basket in the instant pot.
3. Put in water to immerse contents.
4. Secure the lid. Cook on high pressure five minutes.
5. When done, depressurize swiftly.
6. Remove steamer basket. Discard cooked produce.
7. Let flavored water cool. Chill completely and serve.

NUTRITIONAL INFO: Calories: 209 ,Fat: 1g ,Carbohydrates: 51g ,Protein: 2g

MANGO TOMATO SMOOTHIE

Time To Prepare: five minutes

Time to Cook: 0 minutes

Yield: Servings 4

INGREDIENTS:

- 1 cup almond milk
- 2 cups chopped cilantro
- 2 cups pineapple chunks

* 2 mangoes, peeled, pitted
* 4 Campari tomatoes, chopped
* 6 cups fresh baby spinach

DIRECTIONS:

1. Combine all ingredients into a blender and blend until the desired smoothness is achieved.
2. Pour into 4 tall glasses before you serve.

NUTRITIONAL INFO: Calories: 395 kcal ,Protein: 13.1 g ,Fat: 8.19 g ,Carbohydrates: 73.65 g

PARSLEY GINGER GREEN JUICE

Time To Prepare: five minutes

Time to Cook: 0 minutes

Yield: Servings 2

INGREDIENTS:

* 2 cucumbers, chopped
* 2 green apples, cored
* 2 lemons, peeled, halved
* 4 cups chopped parsley
* 4 cups chopped spinach
* 4 inches fresh ginger, peeled, cut
* 6 stalks celery, chopped

DIRECTIONS:

1. Juice together all the ingredients in a juicer.
2. Pour into 2 glasses before you serve.

NUTRITIONAL INFO: Calories: 239 kcal ,Protein: 10.74 g ,Fat: 5.08 g ,Carbohydrates: 44.86 g

MIXED FRUIT & NUT MILKSHAKE

Time To Prepare: five minutes

Time to Cook: 0 minutes

Yield: Servings 2

INGREDIENTS:

* 1 tbsp. of honey
* 1/2 cup of almond milk
* 1½ grapefruit; peeled and chopped
* 1/2½ inch piece of ginger, minced
* 12 strawberries
* 2 tbsp. of chopped almonds
* juice of 1 orange

DIRECTIONS:

1. Put everything but the strawberries in a blender until the desired smoothness is achieved.
2. Put in in the strawberries and blend until pureed, serving in a tall glass.

NUTRITIONAL INFO: Calories: 140 kcal ,Protein: 5.89 g ,Fat: 5.84 g ,Carbohydrates: 17.36 g

PEACH AND RASPBERRY LEMONADE

Time To Prepare: five minutes

Time to Cook: five minutes

Yield: Servings 4

INGREDIENTS:

- ½ cup fresh raspberries
- 1 cup fresh peaches, chopped
- Water to cover ingredients
- Zest and juice of 1 lemon

DIRECTIONS:

1. Put ingredients in mesh basket for instant pot. Put in pot.
2. Put in water to barely cover the fruit.
3. Secure the lid. Cook on high pressure five minutes.
4. When done, depressurize swiftly.
5. Remove steamer basket. Discard cooked produce.
6. Let flavored water cool. Chill completely before you serve.

NUTRITIONAL INFO: Calories: 77 ,Fat: 0g ,Carbohydrates: 19g ,Protein: 0g

PEACH MAPLE SMOOTHIE

Time To Prepare: ten minutes

Time to Cook: 0 minutes

Yield: Servings 1

INGREDIENTS:

- 1 cup fat-free yogurt
- 1 cup ice
- 2 tbsp. maple syrup
- 4 big peaches, peeled and chopped

DIRECTIONS:

1. Put in everything to a blender jug.
2. Cover the jug firmly.
3. Blend until the desired smoothness is achieved. Serve and enjoy!

NUTRITIONAL INFO: Calories: 125 ,Fat: 0.4 g ,Protein: 5.6 g ,Carbohydrates: 8 g ,Fiber: 2.3 g

PEACHY KEEN SMOOTHIE

Time To Prepare: five minutes

Time to Cook: 0 minutes

Yield: Servings 2

INGREDIENTS:

- 1 ½ cups of frozen peaches
- 1 cup of almond milk
- 1 small frozen banana
- 2 tbsp. of raw hemp seeds
- 6 to 8 ice cubes
- Pinch of ground ginger

DIRECTIONS:

1. Mix the smoothie ingredients in your high-speed blender.
2. Pulse the ingredients a few times to cut them up.
3. Combine the mixture on the highest speed setting for thirty to 60 seconds.
4. Pour into glasses and serve.

NUTRITIONAL INFO: Calories: 388 kcal ,Protein: 10.59 g ,Fat: 11.93 g ,Carbohydrates: 64.08 g

PINEAPPLE & GINGER JUICE

Time To Prepare: five minutes

Time to Cook: 0 minutes

Yield: Servings 2

INGREDIENTS:

- 2 apples, cored, chopped
- 2 cucumbers, chopped
- 2 cups chopped pineapple
- 2 cups spinach
- 2 inches ginger, peeled, cut
- 2 lemons, peeled, halved
- 8 celery stalks, chopped

DIRECTIONS:

1. Juice together all the ingredients in a juicer.
2. Pour into 2 glasses before you serve.

NUTRITIONAL INFO: Calories: 339 kcal ,Protein: 7.44 g ,Fat: 4.23 g ,Carbohydrates: 75.38 g

CEREAL CHIA CHIPS

Time To Prepare: ten minutes

Time to Cook: thirty minutes

Yield: Servings 10

INGREDIENTS:

- ¼-cup rolled oats, gluten-free
- ½-cup maple syrup
- ½-cup white quinoa, uncooked
- ¾-cup pecans, chopped
- 2-Tbsps chia seeds
- 2-Tbsps coconut oil
- 2-Tbsps coconut sugar
- A pinch of sea salt (not necessary)

DIRECTIONS:

1. Preheat the oven to 325°F. Coat a baking pan using parchment paper.
2. Mix in the first six ingredients in a mixing container. Mix thoroughly until meticulously blended. Set aside.
3. Pour the oil and syrup in a small deep cooking pan placed on moderate to low heat. Heat the mixture for about three minutes, stirring once in a while.
4. Fold in the dry ingredients; stir thoroughly to coat completely.
5. Pour the mixture in the baking pan, and spread to a uniform layer using a spoon.
6. Place the pan in your oven. Bake for fifteen minutes. Turn the pan around to cook uniformly. Bake for 8-ten minutes until the mixture turns golden brown.
7. Allow cooling completely before breaking the chips into bite-size pieces.

NUTRITIONAL INFO: Calories: 157 ,Fat: 5.2g ,Protein: 7.8g S ,Sodium: 25mg ,Total Carbohydrates: 22.1g ,Fiber: 2.5g ,Net Carbohydrates: 19.6g

CHEWY BLACKBERRY LEATHER

Time To Prepare: fifteen minutes

Time to Cook: 5-6 hours

Yield: Servings 8

INGREDIENTS:

- ¼ cup of raw honey
- 1 tbsp. of fresh mint leaves
- 1 tsp. of ground cinnamon
- 1/8 tsp. of fresh lemon juice
- 2 cups of fresh blackberries

DIRECTIONS:

1. Set the oven to 170F. Coat baking sheet using parchment paper.
2. Use a food processor to put all ingredients and pulse till smooth.

3. Take the mixture onto the readied baking sheet and, using the backside of a spoon, smooth the top.
4. Bake for approximately 5-6 hours.
5. Chop the leather into equal-sized strips.
6. Now, roll each rectangle to make fruit rolls.

NUTRITIONAL INFO: Calories: 49 ,Fat: 0.2g ,Carbohydrates: 12.5g ,Protein: 0.6g ,Fiber: 2.1g

CHIA CASHEW CREAM

Time To Prepare: 2 hours and five minutes

Time to Cook: 0 minutes

Yield: Servings 1

INGREDIENTS:
- ¼-cup quinoa, cooked
- ¼-tsp vanilla powder
- ¾-cup cashew milk
- 2-Tbsps chia seeds
- 2-Tbsps hemp hearts
- 2-Tbsps maple syrup or a dash of liquid stevia
- A pinch of cinnamon

DIRECTIONS:
1. Mix all the ingredients in a jar. Mix thoroughly until meticulously blended. Cover the jar and place in your fridge for about two hours.
2. To serve, top with your desired toppings.

NUTRITIONAL INFO: Calories: 258 ,Fat: 8.6g ,Protein: 12.9g ,Sodium: 123mg ,Total Carbohydrates: 34.2g ,Fiber: 2g ,Net Carbohydrates: 32.2g

COCO CHERRY BAKE-LESS BARS

Time To Prepare: ten minutes

Time to Cook: 0 minutes

Yield: Servings 6

INGREDIENTS:
- ¼-cup pure maple syrup
- ⅓-cup coconut, unsweetened and shredded
- ⅓-cup dried cherries or cranberries
- ⅓-cup ground flaxseed
- ½-cup almond butter
- 1-cup old-fashioned oats
- 1-Tbsp almond milk

- 1-Tbsp vanilla extract
- 3-scoops vanilla plant-based Protein powder

DIRECTIONS:

1. Coat a loaf pan using parchment paper.
2. Mix in the first four ingredients in your blender. Blend until the mixture becomes powdery.
3. Move the mixture to a mixing container. Put in in all the rest of the ingredients. Mix thoroughly until meticulously blended.
4. Put the mixture in the pan, and press down onto a consistently flat surface.
5. Freeze for thirty minutes before cutting into six bars.

NUTRITIONAL INFO: Calories: 193 ,Fat: 6.4g ,Protein: 9.6g ,Sodium: 200mg ,Total Carbohydrates: 27.1g ,Fiber: 3g ,Net Carbohydrates: 24.1g

COCONUT PORRIDGE

Time To Prepare: twenty minutes

Time to Cook: ten minutes

Yield: Servings 2

INGREDIENTS:

- 1 tbsp. coconut oil
- 1 tsp cinnamon
- 1 vanilla bean
- 2 cups oats
- 2 tbsp. maple syrup
- 2 tsp ginger
- 2 tsp turmeric
- 330ml vaporized coconut milk
- 750 ml of water
- Coconut milk
- Fresh, shredded coconut (for serving)

DIRECTIONS:

1. Mix 750 ml water and turmeric in a container. Allow it to sit for about ten minutes.
2. Combine all ingredients apart from coconut milk and shredded coconut in a deep cooking pan.
3. Heat it on medium heat while stirring continuously, and cook for eight minutes.
4. Allow it to cool for about ten minutes.
5. Split into serving bowls.
6. Put in coconut milk and shredded coconut on top.
7. Put in some extra cinnamon to your taste.
8. Eat warm.

NUTRITIONAL INFO: Calories: 417 kcal ,Protein: 20.63 g ,Fat: 16.8 g ,Carbohydrates: 83.03 g

COTTAGE CHEESE WITH APPLE SAUCE

Time To Prepare: five minutes

Time to Cook: 0 minutes

Yield: Servings 2

INGREDIENTS:

- ½ teaspoon cinnamon powder
- 5-6 tablespoons cottage cheese
- two to three tablespoons applesauce or more if required

DIRECTIONS:

1. Split the cottage cheese into 2 bowls.
2. Spread applesauce over the cottage cheese.
3. Drizzle ¼ teaspoon cinnamon powder on each before you serve.

NUTRITIONAL INFO: Calories: 79 kcal ,Protein: 8.09 g ,Fat: 3.45 g ,Carbohydrates: 3.92 g

CUCUMBER ROLLS HORS D'OEUVRES

Time To Prepare: twenty minutes

Time to Cook: 0 minutes

Yield: Servings 8-10

INGREDIENTS:

- ¼ cup fresh dill, finely chopped
- ½ cup capers
- ½ cup fresh parsley + extra to decorate, finely chopped
- 1 teaspoon Himalayan pink salt
- 2 big organic English cucumbers or 4 normal cucumbers
- 5-6 ripe avocadoes, peeled, pitted, mashed
- For the avocado spread:
- Freshly cracked pepper to taste

DIRECTIONS:

1. Peel the cucumbers and cut thin slices along the length on a mandolin slicer.
2. Put the cucumber slices on your countertop.
3. To make the avocado spread: Put in all the ingredients of avocado spread into a container and stir until well blended.
4. Spread the avocado mixture uniformly and thinly on the cucumber slices.
5. Begin rolling from one of the shorter ends to the other end and place on a serving platter with its seam side facing down.
6. Repeat the above step with the rest of the cucumber slices.
7. Serve instantly as the cucumbers tend to get soggy after a while.

NUTRITIONAL INFO: Calories: 227 kcal ,Protein: 3.77 g ,Fat: 19.88 g ,Carbohydrates: 12.99 g

CUCUMBER YOGURT

Time To Prepare: five minutes

Time to Cook: 0 minutes

Yield: Servings 1

INGREDIENTS:

- 1 cup cucumbers, skin removed and chopped in chunks
- 1 teaspoon fresh dill, chopped fine
- 1/4 cup fat-free Greek yogurt
- 2 tablespoons chopped cashews
- 2 teaspoons fresh-squeezed lemon juice

DIRECTIONS:

1. Peel and cut the cucumbers, then put them in a container.
2. Put in the cashews, yogurt, lemon juice, and dill.
3. Mix thoroughly, grab a spoon, and enjoy.

NUTRITIONAL INFO: Calories: 300 kcal ,Protein: 11.35 g ,Fat: 23.55 g ,Carbohydrates: 14.13 g

DELECTABLE COOKIES

Time To Prepare: twenty minutes

Time to Cook: fifteen-twenty minutes

Yield: Servings 6

INGREDIENTS:

- 1 cup of almonds
- ¼ cup of arrowroot flour
- 1 tbsp. of coconut flour
- 1 tsp. ground turmeric
- Salt, to taste
- Freshly ground black pepper, to taste
- 1 organic egg
- ¼ cup of olive oil
- 3 tbsp. of raw honey
- 1 tsp. of organic vanilla extract
- 1 1/3 cups of almond flour

DIRECTIONS:

1. Use a food processor to put the almonds and pulse till chopped roughly
2. Move the chopped almonds in a big container.

3. Place the flours and spices and mix thoroughly.
4. In another container, put the rest of the ingredients then beat till well blended.
5. Put the flour mixture into the egg mixture and mix till well blended.
6. Position a plastic wrap over the cutting board.
7. Put the dough over the cutting board.
8. Use your hands to pat into approximately 1-inch thick circle.
9. Gently chop the circle in 6 wedges.
10. Set the scones onto a cookie sheet in a single layer.
11. Bake for approximately fifteen-20 minutes.

NUTRITIONAL INFO: Calories: 335 ,Fat: 27.7g ,Carbohydrates: 17.6g ,Protein: 9g ,Fiber: 4.8g

DRIED DATES & TURMERIC TRUFFLES

Time To Prepare: fifteen minutes

Time to Cook: 0 minutes

Yield: Servings 4

INGREDIENTS:

- ¼-tsp black pepper
- ⅓ -cup walnuts
- ½-cup rolled oats
- ¾-cup dates, pitted
- 1-Tbsp turmeric powder + more for rolling

DIRECTIONS:

1. Mix in all the ingredients, excluding the dates in a food processor. Blend until meticulously blended.
2. Put in the dates progressively until forming into the dough.
3. Shape and roll balls from the mixture. Roll each ball with the additional turmeric powder until coating fully.
4. Store the truffles in an airtight jar until ready to serve.

NUTRITIONAL INFO: Calories: 95 ,Fat: 3.1g ,Protein: 4.7g ,Sodium: 62mg ,Total Carbohydrates: 13.8g ,Fiber: 2g ,Net Carbohydrates: 11.8g

EASY GUACAMOLE

Time To Prepare: ten minutes

Time to Cook: 0 minutes

Yield: Servings 3

INGREDIENTS:

- ½ Teaspoon Sea Salt
- 1 Teaspoon Garlic Powder

- 4 Avocados, Halved & Pitted

DIRECTIONS:

1. Scoop your avocado flesh out, placing it in a container.
2. Put in in your salt and garlic powder mashing until it's creamy. You can place in your fridge it, and it'll keep for two days.

NUTRITIONAL INFO: Calories: 358 ,Protein: 7.3 Grams ,Fat: 32.2 Grams ,Carbohydrates: 13.7 Grams

EASY PEASY GINGER DATE

Time To Prepare: twenty minutes

Time to Cook: ten minutes

Yield: Servings 8

INGREDIENTS:

- ¼ cup Almond milk
- ¾ cup Dates
- 1 or 1 ½ cup Almonds or almond flour
- 1 tsp. Ground ginger

DIRECTIONS:

1. Preheat your oven to 350ºF.
2. If you're using fresh almonds, put it through a blender to turn it to almond flour. Blitz for a couple of minutes or so until it looks and feels smooth.
3. Do not blitz for too long, or you might end up making nut butter. Now that you have your almond powder put it in a container and set it aside.
4. Pour the dates and almond milk into your blender and pulse for five minutes. If it doesn't resemble a paste, pulse for another two minutes.
5. Pour in the ground ginger and almond flour. Pulse for three to four minutes to combine.
6. Place the mixture to a baking dish and bake for approximately twenty minutes.
7. Take out of the oven and leave to cool before cutting into bits.
8. Serve or store.

NUTRITIONAL INFO: Calories: 55 kcal ,Protein: 1.24 g ,Fat: 0.99 g ,Carbohydrates: 11.24 g

ENERGETIC OAT BARS

Time To Prepare: ten minutes

Time to Cook: twenty-five minutes

Yield: Servings 6

INGREDIENTS:

- ½ cup of gluten-free rolled oats
- ¾ cup fresh blueberries

- 1 peeled and mashed banana
- 1 tbsp. of chopped walnuts
- 1 tbsp. of fresh pomegranate juice
- 1 tbsp. of sunflower seeds
- 2 tbsp. of flax seeds
- 2 tbsp. of pitted and chopped finely dates
- 2 tbsp. of raisins

DIRECTIONS:

1. Set the oven to 350F. Lightly, oil an 8-inch baking dish.
2. In a huge mixing container, put all ingredients and mix till well blended.
3. Put the mixture into the readied baking dish uniformly.
4. Bake for approximately twenty-five minutes. Remove from the oven then cool.
5. Using a knife, split the bars into the size your desired pieces then serve.

NUTRITIONAL INFO: Calories: 88 ,Fat: 2.3g ,Carbohydrates: 18.2g ,Protein: 2.3g ,Fiber: 2.8g

MANDARIN COTTAGE CHEESE

Time To Prepare: five minutes

Time to Cook: 0 minutes

Yield: Servings 1

INGREDIENTS:

- ½ cup canned mandarin oranges
- ½ cup low-fat cottage cheese
- 1 ½ tablespoons slivered almonds

DIRECTIONS:

1. Put the cottage cheese in a container.
2. Drain the mandarin oranges, put them atop the cottage cheese, and drizzle with almonds.

NUTRITIONAL INFO: Calories: 360 kcal ,Protein: 26.24 g ,Fat: 21.37 g ,Carbohydrates: 15.22 g

MINI PEPPER NACHOS

Time To Prepare: five minutes

Time to Cook: ten minutes

Yield: Servings 8

INGREDIENTS:

- .25 tsp. Red pepper flakes
- .5 cup Tomato, chopped

- .5 tsp. Oregano
- 1 tbsp. Chili powder
- 1 tsp. Cumin, ground
- 1 tsp. Garlic powder
- 1 tsp. Paprika
- 16 oz. Ground beef
- 16 oz. Mini peppers, seeded, halved
- 5 tsp. Pepper
- 5 tsp. Salt
- cup Cheddar cheese, shredded

DIRECTIONS:

1. Mix seasonings together in a container.
2. On moderate heat, brown the meat, be sure all the clumps are broken up.
3. Stir in the spices and continue to sauté until the seasoning has gone through all of the meat.
4. Heat the oven to 400F.
5. Put the peppers in a single line. They can touch.
6. Coat with the beef mix.
7. Drizzle with cheese.
8. Bake for minimum ten minutes or until cheese has melted.
9. Pull out of the oven and top with the toppings.

NUTRITIONAL INFO: Calories: 240 kcal ,Protein: 11.01 g ,Fat: 18.2 g ,Carbohydrates: 9.49 g

MUSHROOM CHIPS

Time To Prepare: ten minutes

Time to Cook: 45-60 minutes

Yield: Servings 2-4

INGREDIENTS:

- 16 ounces of king oyster mushrooms
- 2 tablespoons ghee
- Kosher salt and ground pepper to taste

DIRECTIONS:

1. Set the oven to 300F, then line two cookie sheets using parchment paper.
2. Cut every mushroom in half along the length, then cut with a mandolin into 1/8 inch slices or strips. Put them on cookie sheets with some room in between. Melt the ghee and brush it over the mushrooms, then flavor with the salt and pepper.
3. Bake for minimum 45 minutes to an hour, until they are completely crunchy. Store in airtight containers.

NUTRITIONAL INFO: Calories: 62 kcal ,Protein: 5.58 g ,Fat: 2 g ,Carbohydrates: 7.97 g

OLIVE AND TOMATO BALLS

Time To Prepare: ten minutes

Time to Cook: thirty-five minutes

Yield: Servings 5

INGREDIENTS:
- .25 cup Coconut oil
- .25 tsp. Salt
- .5 cup Cream cheese
- 2 cloves Garlic, crushed
- 2 tbsp. Basil, chopped
- 2 tbsp. Oregano, chopped
- 2 tbsp. Thyme, chopped
- 4 Kalamata olives, pitted
- 4 pcs. Sun-dried tomatoes, drained
- 5 tbsp. Parmesan cheese, grated
- Black pepper (as you wish)

DIRECTIONS:
1. Cut the coconut oil, put in it to a small mixing container with the cream cheese, and allow them to tenderize for approximately 30 minutes. Mash together and mix thoroughly to blend.
2. Put in in the Kalamata olives and sun-dried tomatoes and mix thoroughly before you put in in the herbs and seasonings. Mix meticulously before placing the mixing container in your fridge to allow the results to solidify.
3. Once it has solidified, make the mixture into a total of 5 balls using an ice cream scoop. Roll each of the finished balls into the parmesan cheese before plating.
4. Stored the extra's in your refrigerator in an air-tight container for maximum 7 days.

NUTRITIONAL INFO: Calories: 212 kcal ,Protein: 4.77 g ,Fat: 20.75 g ,Carbohydrates: 3.13 g

OVEN CRISP SWEET POTATO

Time To Prepare: ten minutes

Time to Cook: twenty minutes

Yield: Servings 2

INGREDIENTS:
- 1 moderate-sized sweet potato, raw
- 1 teaspoon coconut oil
- 1 teaspoon sugar

DIRECTIONS:
1. Preheat your oven to 160C.
2. Using a mandolin slicer or a peeler, slice the sweet potato into thin chips or strips. Rinse and pat dry.
3. Sprinkle the coconut oil over the potatoes. Toss until all chips are coated.

4. Position in an oven baking sheet. Bake for about ten minutes. Check the crispiness. If it is not that crunchy enough, bake for an extra five or 1o minutes or until the chips attain the crispiness desired.
5. Take out the crunchy sweet potatoes. Drizzle with sugar before you serve.

NUTRITIONAL INFO: Calories: 123 kcal ,Protein: 4.23 g ,Fat: 5.39 g ,Carbohydrates: 14.63 g

PALEO GINGER SPICED MIXED NUTS

Time To Prepare: five minutes

Time to Cook: forty minutes

Yield: Servings 8

INGREDIENTS:

- ½ tsp. Fine sea salt
- ½ tsp. Vietnamese cinnamon
- 1 tsp. Grated fresh ginger
- 2 cups Mix nuts; Cashew, goji berries, raw almonds, pumpkin seeds, etc.
- 2 Large Egg,
- Coconut oil spray
- Egg whites

DIRECTIONS:

1. Prepare the oven by preheating to 250°F.
2. Whisk egg whites in a container until it gets fluffy. Pour in sea salt, grated ginger, and Vietnamese cinnamon. Whisk until it's one big mix.
3. Pour in the mixed nuts and stir to combine.
4. Coat the parchment-lined baking sheet with coconut oil spray and spread the nut mixture all across the baking sheet.
5. Allow it to bake for approximately twenty minutes, rotate the sheet then bake for another twenty minutes.
6. Take off the baking sheet from the oven and leave to cool.
7. Once it's fully cool and hard, break them into bits with clean hands.
8. Serve or store.

NUTRITIONAL INFO: Calories: 212 kcal ,Protein: 6.92 g ,Fat: 17.3 g ,Carbohydrates: 10.05 g

PARTY-TIME CHICKEN NUGGETS

Time To Prepare: ten minutes

Time to Cook: twenty-five minutes

Yield: Servings 6

INGREDIENTS:

- ½ cup tapioca flour

- ½ tsp. of garlic powder
- ½ tsp. of onion powder
- ½ tsp. of paprika
- 1½ cups of blanched almond flour
- 2 (6-ounce) grass-fed skinless, boneless chicken breasts
- 2 big organic eggs
- Freshly ground black pepper, to taste
- Salt, to taste

DIRECTIONS:

1. Set the oven to 400F then grease a big baking sheet.
2. With a rolling pin, roll the chicken breasts to a uniform thickness.
3. Cut each breast into bite-sized pieces.
4. In a shallow dish, crack the eggs and beat thoroughly.
5. In another shallow dish, combine flours and spices.
6. Immerse the chicken nuggets in beaten eggs.
7. Then roll in flour mixture completely.
8. Position the nuggets onto the readied baking sheet in a single layer.
9. Bake for approximately 10-twelve minutes, turning once after five minutes.

NUTRITIONAL INFO: Calories: 312 ,Fat: 17.8g ,Carbohydrates: 15.4g ,Protein: 23.6g ,Fiber: 3.2g

PEANUT BUTTER AND HONEY OAT BARS

Time To Prepare: ten minutes

Time to Cook: twenty-five minutes

Yield: Servings 18

INGREDIENTS:

- ¼ cup honey
- ¼ cup honey roasted peanuts, chopped
- ¼ teaspoon cinnamon powder
- ¼ teaspoon vanilla extract
- 1 cup oats
- 2 teaspoons coconut oil
- 3 tablespoons peanut butter

DIRECTIONS:

1. Coat a small baking pan using a parchment paper such that the parchment paper is hanging over the sides of the baking pan.
2. Put in honey, oil, and peanut butter into a microwave-safe container. Microwave on High for around 20 - half a minute or until the peanut butter melts completely. If it takes longer than half a minute, stir and cook in increments of 10 seconds, stirring every time.
3. Remove from the microwave and put in the remaining ingredients. Mix thoroughly and pour into the readied baking pan. Spread the mixture and press using a spatula.

4. Bake in a preheated oven 300° F for approximately twenty minutes or until the top is light brown.
5. Take out of the oven and press once once more.
6. Cool for a while and slice.
7. Cool thoroughly before you serve.
8. Move leftover bars into an airtight container. Place in your fridge until use.

NUTRITIONAL INFO: Calories: 44 kcal ,Protein: 1.47 g ,Fat: 1.69 g ,Carbohydrates: 8.06 g

PROTEIN-PACKED CROQUETTES

Time To Prepare: ten minutes

Time to Cook: five minutes

Yield: Servings 12

INGREDIENTS:

- ¼ cup of chopped fresh cilantro leaves
- ¼ cup plus 1 tbsp. of olive oil, divided
- ¼ tsp. of ground turmeric
- ½ cup of thawed frozen peas
- ½ tsp. of paprika
- 1 cup of cooked quinoa
- 2 big peeled and mashed boiled potatoes
- 2 minced garlic cloves
- 2 tsp. of ground cumin
- Freshly ground black pepper, to taste
- Salt, to taste

DIRECTIONS:

1. In a frying pan, heat 1 tbsp. of oil on moderate heat.
2. Put in peas and garlic and sauté for approximately one minute.
3. Move the peas mixture into a big container.
4. Put rest of the ingredients then mix till well blended.
5. Make equal sized oblong shaped patties from the mixture.
6. In a huge frying pan, warm remaining oil on moderate to high heat.
7. Put in croquettes in batches and fry for approximately 4 minutes per side.

NUTRITIONAL INFO: Calories: 152 ,Fat: 6.9g ,Carbohydrates: 20.1g ,Protein: 3.5g ,Fiber: 2.9g

ROASTED BEETS

Time To Prepare: ten minutes

Time to Cook: 35-45 minutes

Yield: Servings 6

INGREDIENTS:

- 1 tablespoon of coconut oil, melted
- 1 teaspoon of salt
- 2 and a ½ pounds of beets, peeled and diced

DIRECTIONS:

1. Preheat your oven to 400°F.
2. Spread the beets onto a baking sheet and sprinkle with melted coconut oil.
3. Put in salt and mix thoroughly.
4. Roast the beets in your oven for 35-45 minutes, until the beets are tender.

NUTRITIONAL INFO: ,Total Carbohydrates: 7g ,Fiber: 2g ,Net Carbohydrates: ,Protein: 1g ,Total Fat: 4g Calories: 59

ROASTED GARLIC CHICKPEAS

Time To Prepare: five minutes

Time to Cook: twenty minutes

Yield: Servings 2

INGREDIENTS:

- 1 Teaspoon Garlic Powder
- 1 Teaspoon Sea Salt
- 2 Tablespoons Olive Oil
- 4 Cups Cooked Chickpeas, Rinsed, Drained & Dried
- Black Pepper to Taste

DIRECTIONS:

1. Begin by heating the oven to 400.
2. Spread your chickpeas on a baking sheet, coating them with your olive oil.
3. Bake of 20 minutes, ensuring to stir them at the ten-minute mark.
4. Put your hot chickpeas in a container, seasoning before securing them in an airtight container. They'll keep at room temperature for maximum two days.

NUTRITIONAL INFO: Calories: 150 ,Protein: 6 Grams ,Fat: 5 Grams ,Carbohydrates: 21 Grams

SALMON & AVOCADO TOAST

Time To Prepare: ten minutes

Time to Cook: five minutes

Yield: Servings 1

INGREDIENTS:

- ¼ tsp red pepper
- ½ avocado

- 1 tsp lemon juice
- 2 slices of gluten-free bread
- oz. pink salmon (wild)
- salt and pepper - to taste

DIRECTIONS:

1. Cut the avocado.
2. Toast the bread to your taste.
3. Combine the salmon and lemon juice.
4. When the toast is ready, lay avocado slices onto it.
5. Cover with salmon.
6. Put in some red pepper, salt, and pepper to your taste.
7. Feel free to put the other ingredients you prefer (tomatoes, onions)
8. Enjoy your salmon snack!

NUTRITIONAL INFO: Calories: 481 kcal ,Protein: 28.08 g ,Fat: 27.52 g ,Carbohydrates: 33 g

SALT & VINEGAR KALE CRISPS

Time To Prepare: five minutes

Time to Cook: 20-twenty-five minutes

Yield: Servings 2

INGREDIENTS:

- 1 Teaspoon Sea Salt, Fine
- 2 Tablespoon Apple Cider Vinegar
- 2 Tablespoons Olive Oil
- 4 Cups Kale, Torn into 2 Inch Pieces

DIRECTIONS:

1. Begin by heating the oven to 350. Get out a container, and mix all of your ingredients.
2. Put your kale on a baking sheet, baking for twenty to twenty-five minutes. Toss midway through this time.
3. Put at room temperature in an airtight container. They'll keep for two days.

NUTRITIONAL INFO: Calories: 135 ,Protein: 1 Gram ,Fat: 14 Grams ,Carbohydrates: 3 Grams

SOFT FLOURLESS COOKIES

Time To Prepare: ten minutes

Time to Cook: twenty-five minutes

Yield: Servings 4

INGREDIENTS:

- ¼ teaspoon of organic vanilla extract

- ¾ cup of shredded unsweetened coconut
- 1 peeled big banana
- Pinch of ground cinnamon

DIRECTIONS:
1. Set the oven to 350F. Coat a cookie sheet with a big greased parchment paper.
2. In a big food processor, put all ingredients and pulse till well blended.
3. Ladle the mixture onto the prepared cookie sheet. Use your hands to flatten the cookies slightly.
4. Bake for minimum twenty-five minutes or till golden brown.

NUTRITIONAL INFO: Calories: 84 ,Fat: 5.1g ,Carbohydrates: 10.1g ,Protein: 0.9g ,Fiber: 2.3g

SPICED NUTS

Time To Prepare: ten minutes

Time to Cook: 10-fifteen minutes

Yield: Servings 2

INGREDIENTS:
- ¼ Cup Pumpkin Puree
- ¼ Cup Sunflower Seeds
- ¼ Teaspoon Garlic Powder
- ¼ Teaspoon Red Pepper Flakes
- ½ Cup Walnuts
- ½ Teaspoon Ground Cumin
- 1 Cup Almonds
- 1 Teaspoon Ground Turmeric

DIRECTIONS:
1. Begin by heating the oven to 350.
2. Mix all ingredients together, and then get out a baking sheet. Spread your nuts over your baking sheet, cooking for ten to fifteen minutes.
3. Allow it to cool well before you store it.

NUTRITIONAL INFO: Calories: 180 ,Protein: 6 Grams ,Fat: 16 Grams ,Carbohydrates: 7 Grams

SPICY BEAN DIP

Time To Prepare: ten minutes

Time to Cook: 0 minutes

Yield: Servings 3

INGREDIENTS:
- ¼ Teaspoon Ground Cumin
- ¼ Teaspoon Sea Salt

- 1 Tablespoon Apple Cider Vinegar
- 1 Teaspoon Lime Juice, Fresh
- 14 Ounce Can Black Beans, Drained & Rinsed
- 14 Ounce Can Kidney Beans, Drained & Rinsed
- 2 Cherry Tomatoes
- 2 Cloves Garlic
- 2 Tablespoons Water
- 2 Teaspoon Honey, Raw
- Black Pepper to Taste
- Pinch Cayenne Pepper

DIRECTIONS:

1. Mix all of your ingredients in a food processor, and blend until it's smooth.
2. Cover, and place in your fridge before you serve.

NUTRITIONAL INFO: Calories: 166 ,Protein: 9.4 Grams ,Fat: 0.6 Grams ,Carbohydrates: 34.2 Grams

SWEET POTATO MUFFINS

Time To Prepare: fifteen minutes

Time to Cook: 20-twenty-five minutes

Yield: Servings 12

INGREDIENTS:

- ¼ Cup Almond Butter
- ¼ Teaspoon Sea Salt
- ½ Teaspoon Baking Soda
- 1 ½ Cups Rolled Oats
- 1 Cup Almond Milk
- 1 Cup Sweet Potato, Cooked & Pureed
- 1 Egg
- 1 Teaspoon Baking Powder
- 1 Teaspoon Ground Cinnamon
- 1 Teaspoon Vanilla Extract, Pure
- 1/3 Cup Coconut Sugar
- 2 Tablespoons Olive Oil

DIRECTIONS:

1. Begin by heating the oven to 375.
2. Coat your muffin tin with liners, and get out a food processor.
3. Pulse your oats until it forms a course flour. Move it to a small container before setting it to the side.
4. Put in all of your ingredients apart from for the oat flour, blending until the desired smoothness is achieved.
5. Slowly put in in your oat flour, pulsing until it's well blended.

6. Cut between your cupcake liners, and bake for about twenty minutes. Let them cool for minimum five minutes before you serve.

NUTRITIONAL INFO: Calories: 143 ,Protein: 4 Grams ,Fat: 7 Grams ,Carbohydrates: 12 Grams

SWEET SUNUP SEEDS

Time To Prepare: five minutes

Time to Cook: 60 minutes

Yield: Servings 8

INGREDIENTS:

- ¼-cup pure maple syrup
- ¼-cup sunflower oil
- ¼-sesame seeds
- ⅓ -cup honey
- ½-cup flaxseed
- 1-cup dried cranberries
- 1-cup raw pumpkin seeds
- 1-tsp vanilla extract
- 3-tsp cinnamon
- 4-cups rolled oats

DIRECTIONS:

1. Preheat your oven to 350°F. Prepare two units of baking sheets by lining them using parchment paper.
2. In a large-sized mixing container, mix the rolled oats, pumpkin seeds, flaxseed, sesame seeds, and cinnamon. Mix gently until meticulously blended.
3. Pour all the liquid ingredients into the mixture and stir until mixed well.
4. On the baking sheets, spread the mixture uniformly. Place the sheets in your oven. Cook for minimum an hour. While baking, stir the mixture every quarter of an hour to achieve uniform color on its surfaces.
5. Take away the sheets from the oven. Allow cooling completely. Put in the cup of dried cranberries, and mix thoroughly.
6. Store the granola in an airtight container to maintain its freshness and crunchiness.

NUTRITIONAL INFO: Calories: 189 ,Fat: 6.3g ,Protein: 9.4g ,Sodium: 5mg ,Total Carbohydrates: 27.6g ,Fiber: 4g ,Net Carbohydrates: 23.6g

TANGY TURMERIC FLAVORED FLORETS

Time To Prepare: ten minutes

Time to Cook: 55 minutes

Yield: Servings 1

INGREDIENTS:

- 1-head cauliflower, chopped into florets
- 1-Tbsp olive oil
- 1-Tbsp turmeric
- A dash of salt
- A pinch of cumin

DIRECTIONS:

1. Set the oven to 400°F.
2. Combine all ingredients in a baking pan. Mix thoroughly until meticulously blended.
3. Cover the pan using foil. Roast for forty minutes. Take away the foil cover and roast additionally for fifteen minutes.

NUTRITIONAL INFO: Calories: 90 ,Fat: 3g ,Protein: 4.5g ,Sodium: 87mg ,Total Carbohydrates: 16.2g ,Fiber: 5g ,Net Carbohydrates: 11.2g

TOASTED PUMPKIN SEEDS

Time To Prepare: five minutes

Time to Cook: thirty minutes

Yield: Servings 2-4

INGREDIENTS:

- ½ teaspoon extra virgin olive oil
- 1 teaspoon salt
- 1 to 2 cups pumpkin seeds
- Sea salt
- Water

DIRECTIONS:

1. Put seeds in a deep cooking pan and cover with water. Put in salt.
2. Bring it to its boiling point and boil for about ten minutes.
3. Simmer uncovered for ten more minutes. This makes the seeds very crunchy when baked. Drain the seeds and pat dry using a paper towel.
4. Coat a baking sheet using parchment paper and spread out the seeds in a single layer.
5. Sprinkle with salt, then bake in an oven at 325F for minimum ten minutes, stirring midway through.
6. Cool, then store in an airtight container.

NUTRITIONAL INFO: Calories: 192 kcal ,Protein: 10.41 g ,Fat: 16.23 g ,Carbohydrates: 4.34 g

TOFU PUDDING

Time To Prepare: ten minutes

Time to Cook: 0 minutes

Yield: Servings 4

INGREDIENTS:

- 1 cup strawberries
- 1 teaspoon honey
- 1 teaspoon pumpkin pie spice
- 1 teaspoon vanilla
- 12 ounces silken tofu, softened and well-drained
- 2 scoops of Protein powder
- 3/4 cup blueberries
- 4 almonds
- Fresh mint leaves

DIRECTIONS:

1. Combine the tofu and Protein powder in a blender until thoroughly combined.
2. Put in the blueberries, strawberries, honey, pumpkin pie spice, and vanilla. Blend until the desired smoothness is achieved.
3. Cover and put on the refrigerator to chill for minimum 2 hours.
4. Ladle into four dessert bowls and top with an almond and a mint leaf before you serve.

NUTRITIONAL INFO: Calories: 371 kcal ,Protein: 23.31 g ,Fat: 21.1 g ,Carbohydrates: 27.17 g

TURMERIC CHICKPEA CAKES

Time To Prepare: twenty minutes

Time to Cook: thirty minutes

Yield: Servings 8

INGREDIENTS:

- ½ cup fresh parsley, minced
- 1 teaspoon cayenne pepper, to taste (not necessary)
- 1 teaspoon salt or to taste
- 2 cans (15oz.) chickpeas, washed, drained
- 2 small onions, minced
- 2 teaspoons turmeric powder
- 4 cloves garlic, minced
- 4 tablespoons cornstarch
- 8-10 tablespoons chickpea flour
- Avocado dipping sauce to serve
- Freshly ground pepper to taste
- Grapeseed oil to fry

DIRECTIONS:

1. Put a frying pan on moderate heat. Put in a little oil. When the oil is heated, put onion and garlic and sauté until translucent. Remove the heat and cool to room temperature.
2. Put in chickpeas into the food processor container and pulse until very finely chopped.

3. Put in the onion mixture, salt, pepper, cayenne pepper, and turmeric powder and pulse again until well blended.
4. Move into a container. Put in parsley and mix thoroughly.
5. Make small balls of the mixture (of approximately 1 inch diameter) and mould into patties. Put chickpea flour on a plate.
6. Put a nonstick pan on moderate heat. Put in a little oil and swirl the pan so that the oil spreads.
7. Immerse the patties in the chickpea flour and place a few on the pan. Cook in batches.
8. Cook until the underside is golden brown. Flip then cook the other side till it's golden brown.
9. Repeat steps 6-8 to fry the rest of the patties.
10. Serve with avocado dipping sauce.

NUTRITIONAL INFO: Calories: 154 kcal ,Protein: 7.32 g ,Fat: 2.85 g ,Carbohydrates: 25.43 g

TURMERIC COCONUT FLOUR MUFFINS

Time To Prepare: five minutes

Time to Cook: twenty-five minutes

Yield: Servings 8

INGREDIENTS:
- ½ cup Unsweetened coconut milk
- ½ tsp. Baking soda
- ½ tsp. Ginger powder
- ¾ cup & 2 tbsp. Coconut flour
- 1 tsp. Vanilla extract
- 1/3 cup Maple syrup
- 2 tsp. Turmeric
- 6 big Whole eggs
- Pepper and salt

DIRECTIONS:
1. Preheat your oven to 350°F.
2. Coat 8 muffin tins with 8 muffin liners.
3. Whisk eggs, maple syrup, milk, and vanilla extract in a mixing container until the egg begins to make bubbles.
4. In a different container, combine the coconut flour, turmeric powder, pepper, baking soda, ginger powder, and salt.
5. Place the dry mixture into the wet mixture then stir until it's all mixed and thick.
6. Ladle out the batter into prepared muffin tins.
7. Leave to bake for about twenty-five minutes or until it looked golden.
8. Allow the muffins cool for a couple of minutes before transferring them to a rack.

NUTRITIONAL INFO: Calories: 143 kcal ,Protein: 6.18 g ,Fat: 8 g ,Carbohydrates: 11.8 g

TURMERIC GUMMIES

Time To Prepare: five minutes

Time to Cook: 4 hours and ten minutes

Yield: Servings 4

INGREDIENTS:

- ¼ tsp. Ground pepper
- 1 tsp. Ground turmeric
- 3 ½ cups Water
- 6 tbsp. Maple syrup
- 8 tbsp. Unflavored gelatin powder

DIRECTIONS:

1. Combine the ground turmeric, maple syrup, and water in a pot set on moderate heat. Stir continuously for five minutes before removing from heat and pouring in the gelatin powder. Stir using a wooden spoon to dissolve the gelatin.
2. Put back the pan on the heat and stir for another two minutes.
3. Remove the heat and take the mixture to a deep container that you will seal using plastic wrapimmediately after.
4. Place in your fridge the mixture for approximately 4 hours.
5. It must be firm now, cut it into little squares, and serve or store.

NUTRITIONAL INFO: Calories: 123 kcal ,Protein: 2.15 g ,Fat: 1.56 g ,Carbohydrates: 25.67 g

ANTI-INFLAMMATORY SPRING PEA SOUP

Time To Prepare: five minutes

Time to Cook: fifteen minutes

Yield: Servings 6

INGREDIENTS:

- ½ tsp. Black pepper powder
- ½ tsp. ground cumin
- 1 liter Vegetable stock
- 1 medium Chopped onion
- 2 tbsp. Coconut oil
- 2 tsp. Celtic sea salt
- 700 g. Fresh peas
- Chopped flat-leaf parsley
- Chopped mint leaves
- Fresh lemon juice
- Grated nutmeg

- Toasted sunflower seeds

DIRECTIONS:

1. Warm the coconut oil in a pan set on moderate heat.
2. Mix in onions and stir fry for approximately five minutes.
3. Put in the stock and raise the heat. Throw in fresh peas and cook for five minutes. If you're using frozen peas, it should take half the time.
4. Pour in the lemon juice, salt, pepper, herbs, and spices. Stirring continuously
5. Remove the heat and allow it to cool before running it through a food processor to whatever consistency you prefer.
6. Serve with sunflower seed sprinkles and mint or parsley leaves.
7. Enjoy!

NUTRITIONAL INFO: Calories: 115 kcal ,Protein: 5 g ,Fat: 5.91 g ,Carbohydrates: 11.8 g

ANTI-INFLAMMATORY SWEET POTATO SOUP

Time To Prepare: twenty minutes

Time to Cook: thirty minutes

Yield: Servings 8

INGREDIENTS:

- 1 13.66-ounce can lite coconut milk
- 1 big zucchini, cut width-wise
- 1 garlic clove
- 1 liter low-sodium vegetable stock
- 1 tablespoon sweet yellow curry powder
- 1 teaspoon black pepper
- 1 teaspoon cayenne pepper
- 1 teaspoon turmeric
- 1 white onion
- 2 moderate-sized white potatoes,
- 3 moderate-sized sweet potatoes,
- 3/4 tablespoons salt
- 4 cups of hot water
- 4 tablespoons olive oil
- A pinch of cinnamon
- A pinch of cloves

DIRECTIONS:

1. Prepare every one of your vegetables by cutting, cleaning & cubing. Put in a safe spot.

2. To a large pot, include 4 tablespoons of additional virgin olive oil. Allow it to heat up swiftly; at that point, include your white onion. Allow it to sweat for minimum five minutes on low warmth.

3. Put in all your flavoring & garlic. Give it a decent mix; at that point, including the potatoes.

4. Allow these cook on moderate heat for around five minutes to get a pleasant darker shading. Continue blending to abstain from consuming.

5. Put in your stalk & water, warm it to the point of boiling & then stew for around 20-twenty-five minutes. Part of the way through the stewing procedure, include your zucchini.

6. After 20-twenty-five minutes, include your coconut milk. Before pouring the soup to the blender, do a fork content to guarantee your potatoes are cooked.

7. Use your blender to purée the soup. Embellishment with lemon juice, dark pepper & herbs & flavors of your preference.

NUTRITIONAL INFO: Calories: 281 kcal ,Protein: 4.1 g ,Fat: 20.22 g ,Carbohydrates: 23.8 g

BACON & CHEESE SOUP

Time To Prepare: fifteen minutes

Time to Cook: forty minutes

Yield: Servings 6

INGREDIENTS:
- ½ cup sour cream, for serving
- ½ teaspoon cumin
- ½ teaspoon onion powder
- ½ teaspoon paprika
- 1 cup heavy cream
- 1 cup shredded cheddar cheese
- 1 pound of lean ground beef
- 1 tablespoon coconut oil, for cooking
- 1 teaspoon garlic powder
- 1 yellow onion, chopped
- 6 cups beef broth
- 6 slices uncured bacon

DIRECTIONS:
1. Put in the coconut oil to a frying pan and cook the bacon until crunchy. Allow the bacon to cool and cut into little pieces. Set aside.

2. Once cooked, put in the lean ground beef to the same frying pan with the bacon fat and cook until browned.

3. Put in the onions and cook for an extra two to three minutes.

4. Put in all the ingredients minus the bacon, heavy cream, sour cream and cheese to a stockpot and stir. Cook for about twenty-five minutes.

5. Warm the heavy cream, and then put in the warmed cream and cheese and serve with the bacon and a spoonful of sour cream.

BEEF AND VEGGIE SOUP

Time To Prepare: ten minutes

Time to Cook: twenty minutes

Yield: Servings 8

INGREDIENTS:

- ½ cup heavy whipping cream
- ½ cup onion, chopped
- 1 (8 ounces / 227 g) package cream cheese, softened
- 1 pound (454 g) ground beef
- 1 tablespoon ground cumin
- 1 teaspoon chili powder
- 2 (10 ounces / 284 g) cans diced tomatoes and green chiles
- 2 (14.5 ounces / 411 g) cans beef broth
- 2 cloves garlic, minced
- 2 teaspoons salt, or to taste

DIRECTIONS:

1. Position the ground beef, chopped onion, and garlic in a pot, stir until blended well. Cook on moderate to high heat for five to seven minutes or until the beef is thoroughly browned. Stir continuously.
2. Discard the grease extract from the beef, then put in chili powder and cumin, and cook for an extra two minutes. Stir continuously.
3. Put in the cream cheese to the pot and cook for three to five minutes more, then fold in the tomatoes and green chiles, beef broth, heavy whipping cream, and salt, and cook for about ten minutes to cook through. Keep stirring during the cooking.
4. Serve the soup in a big serving container. Allow to stand for a couple of minutes before you serve.

NUTRITIONAL INFO: calories: 288 ,total fat: 24g ,carbs: 5.4g ,protein: 13.4g ,Cholesterol: 85mg ,Sodium: 1310mg

BROCCOLI CHEDDAR & BACON SOUP

Time To Prepare: ten minutes

Time to Cook: ten minutes

Yield: Servings 6

INGREDIENTS:

- ¼ teaspoon black pepper
- ½ teaspoon salt

- ½ white onion, chopped
- 1 cup broccoli florets finely chopped
- 1 cup heavy cream
- 1 cup shredded cheddar cheese
- 2 cloves garlic, chopped
- 2 cups chicken broth
- 3 slices cooked bacon, crumbled for serving

DIRECTIONS:

1. Put in all the ingredients minus the heavy cream, cheddar cheese and bacon to a stockpot on moderate heat.
2. Heat to a simmer and cook for 5 minutes.
3. Warm the cream, and then put in the warm cream and cheddar cheese. Whisk until the desired smoothness is achieved.
4. Serve with crumbled bacon.

NUTRITIONAL INFO: Calories: 220 ,Carbohydrates: 4g ,Fiber: 1g Net ,Carbohydrates: 3g ,Fat: 18g ,Protein: 11g

BROCCOLI SOUP WITH GORGONZOLA CHEESE

Time To Prepare: ten minutes

Time to Cook: thirty minutes

Yield: Servings 4

INGREDIENTS:

- ½ cup 18% cream
- 1 big broccoli, divided into little roses
- 1 flat teaspoon of sweet pepper
- 1 onion, diced
- 1 tablespoon of chopped fresh basil
- 1 tablespoon of chopped parsley
- 1 tablespoon of oil
- 150 g Gorgonzola cheese, diced
- 2 potatoes, peeled and diced
- 4 tablespoons of almond flakes roasted in a dry pan
- 5 garlic cloves, chopped
- 750 ml broth
- a pinch of sugar
- pumpkin oil (not necessary)
- salt and pepper

DIRECTIONS:

1. In a big deep cooking pan, warm the oil on moderate heat, put the onion and garlic, and fry it until the vitrified glass onion.
2. Then put the broccoli with potatoes, pour the broth and cook for approximately fifteen-twenty minutes until the vegetables become tender. Put in basil, parsley, sugar, pepper, and pepper to taste.
3. Put in cheese and cream, and when the cheese dissolves, blend with a blender until the desired smoothness is achieved. Sprinkle with salt and pepper if required.
4. Serve the soup sprinkled with almond flakes and sprinkled with pumpkin oil.

NUTRITIONAL INFO: Calories: 382 kcal ,Protein: 13.06 g ,Fat: 18.93 g ,Carbohydrates: 41.65 g

BROWN RICE AND SHITAKE MISO SOUP WITH SCALLION

Time To Prepare: ten minutes

Time to Cook: forty-five minutes

Yield: Servings 4

INGREDIENTS:

- ½ teaspoon salt
- 1 (1½-inch) piece fresh ginger, peeled and cut
- 1 cup medium-grain brown rice
- 1 cup thinly cut shiitake mushroom caps
- 1 garlic clove, minced
- 1 tablespoon white miso
- 2 scallions, thinly cut
- 2 tablespoons finely chopped fresh cilantro
- 2 tablespoons sesame oil

DIRECTIONS:

1. In a large pot, heat the oil on moderate to high heat.
2. Put in the mushrooms, garlic, and ginger and sauté until the mushrooms start to tenderize, approximately five minutes.
3. Place the rice and stir to uniformly coat with the oil.
4. Put in 2 cups of water and salt and place it to its boiling point.
5. Reduce the heat then cook until the rice is soft, thirty to forty minutes.
6. Use a little of the soup broth to tenderize the miso, then mix it into the pot until well mixed.
7. Stir in the scallions and cilantro, then serve.

NUTRITIONAL INFO: Calories: 265 ,Total Fat: 8g ,Total Carbohydrates: 43g ,Sugar: 2g ,Fiber: 3g ,Protein: 5g ,Sodium: 456mg

BUFFALO SAUCE AND TURKEY SOUP

Time To Prepare: five minutes

Time to Cook: ten minutes

Yield: Servings 4

INGREDIENTS:

- ⅓ cup buffalo sauce
- 2 cups turkey, cooked, shredded
- 3 tablespoons butter, melted
- 4 cups chicken broth
- 4 ounces (113 g) cream cheese
- 4 tablespoons cilantro, chopped
- From The Cupboard:
- Salt and freshly ground black pepper, to taste

DIRECTIONS:

1. Place the buffalo sauce, cream cheese, and melted butter in a blender, and process until the desired smoothness is achieved.
2. Pour the buffalo sauce mixture in a deep cooking pan, and put in the chicken broth. Heat the soup using high heat until hot and nearly boil off but not boil. Keep stirring during the heating.
3. Put in the shredded turkey, and drizzle with salt and black pepper. Cook for five minutes or until the desired smoothness is achieved. Stir continuously.
4. Ladle the soup into a big container and top with chopped cilantro before you serve.

NUTRITIONAL INFO: calories: 409 ,total fat: 29.7g ,net carbs: 9.2g ,protein: 26.4g

BUTTERNUT SQUASH SOUP WITH SHRIMP

Time To Prepare: ten minutes

Time to Cook: twenty minutes

Yield: Servings 4

INGREDIENTS:

- ¼ cup slivered almonds (not necessary)
- ¼ teaspoon freshly ground black pepper
- 1 cup unsweetened almond milk
- 1 garlic clove, cut
- 1 pound cooked peeled shrimp, thawed if required
- 1 small red onion, finely chopped
- 1 teaspoon salt
- 1 teaspoon turmeric
- 2 cups peeled butternut squash cut into ¼-inch dice
- 2 tablespoons finely chopped fresh flat-leaf parsley
- 2 teaspoons grated or minced lemon zest
- 3 cups vegetable broth

- 3 tablespoons unsalted butter

DIRECTIONS:

1. In a large pot, melt the butter on high heat.
2. Put in the onion, garlic, turmeric, salt, and pepper and sauté until the vegetables are tender and translucent, five to seven minutes.
3. Put in the broth and squash and bring to its boiling point.
4. Reduce the heat and cook until the squash has tenderized, approximately five minutes.
5. Put in the shrimp and almond milk and cook until thoroughly heated, approximately 2 minutes.
6. Drizzle with the almonds (if using), parsley, and lemon zest before you serve.

NUTRITIONAL INFO: Calories: 275 ,Total Fat: 12g ,Total Carbohydrates: 12g ,Sugar: 3g ,Fiber: 2g; ,Protein: 30g ,Sodium: 1665mg

CANNELLINI BEAN SOUP

Time To Prepare: twenty-five minutes

Time to Cook: thirty minutes

Yield: Servings 6

INGREDIENTS:

- 1 bunch red Swiss chard
- 1 cannellini beans
- 1 clove garlic (minced)
- 1 onion (chopped)
- 1 tablespoon extra-virgin olive oil
- 1/4 teaspoon nutmeg (grated)
- 1/8 teaspoon red pepper flakes (crushed)
- 2 ounces Parmesan cheese rind
- 2 slices smoked bacon (chopped)
- 2 tablespoons chopped sun-dried tomatoes
- 5 big sage leaves (minced)
- 5 leaves basil (chopped)
- 6 cups chicken broth

DIRECTIONS:

1. Cook the bacon with garlic, onion, nutmeg, and red pepper flakes for five minutes.
2. Pour in beans, chicken broth, sun-dried tomatoes, and Parmesan cheese rind, simmering for about ten minutes.
3. Put in the cut chard and chard leaves into the soup.
4. Simmer and then put in into bowls with a sprinkle of oil and Parmesan cheese.

NUTRITIONAL INFO: Calories: 215 kcal ,Carbohydrates: 23 g ,Fat: 10 g ,Protein: 9.7 g

CARROT BROCCOLI STEW

Time To Prepare: ten minutes

Time to Cook: forty-five minutes

Yield: Servings 3

INGREDIENTS:

- 1 cup Broccoli, florets
- 1 cup Carrots, cut
- 1 cup Heavy Cream
- 3 cups Chicken broth
- Salt and black pepper to taste

DIRECTIONS:

1. Put in florets, cream, carrots, salt, and chicken broth; toss thoroughly. Secure the lid and cook on Meat/Stew mode for forty minutes on High. When ready, do a quick pressure release.
2. Move into serving bowls and drizzle black pepper on top.

NUTRITIONAL INFO: Calories 145 ,Protein: 1.5g ,Carbs: 1.2g

CARROT, GINGER & TURMERIC SOUP

Time To Prepare: fifteen minutes

Time to Cook: forty minutes

Yield: Servings 8

INGREDIENTS:

- ¼ cup full-fat unsweetened coconut milk
- ¾ pound carrots, peeled and chopped
- 1 sweet yellow onion, chopped
- 1 teaspoon ground turmeric
- 2 cloves garlic, chopped
- 2 teaspoons grated ginger
- 6 cups vegetable broth
- Pinch of sea salt & pepper, to taste

DIRECTIONS:

1. Put in all the ingredients minus the coconut milk to a stockpot on moderate heat and bring to its boiling point. Reduce to a simmer and cook for forty minutes or until the carrots are soft.
2. Use an immersion blender and blend the soup until the desired smoothness is achieved. Mix in the coconut milk.
3. Enjoy immediately and freeze any remainings.

NUTRITIONAL INFO: Calories: 73 ,Carbohydrates: 7g ,Fiber: 2g Net ,Carbohydrates: 5g ,Fat: 3g ,Protein: 4g

CAULIFLOWER AND CLAM CHOWDER

Time To Prepare: ten minutes

Time to Cook: ten minutes

Yield: Servings 6

INGREDIENTS:

- ½ teaspoon dried thyme
- 1 small yellow onion
- 1½ cups heavy whipping cream
- 3 (6.5-ounce / 184-g) cans chopped clams
- 3 tablespoons butter
- 4 cups chopped cauliflower
- From the cupboard:
- Salt and freshly ground black pepper, to taste

DIRECTIONS:

1. Split the clams and clam juice into two bowls. Thin the clam juice with water to make 2 cups of juice.
2. Place the onion and butter in an instant pot and press the Sauté bottom, then sauté for a couple of minutes or until the onion is translucent.
3. Put in the clam juice and cauliflower into the instant pot. Place the lid on and press the Manual button, and set the temperature to 375ºF (190ºC), then cook for five minutes.
4. Quick Release the pressure, then open the lid and mix in the heavy cream and clams.
5. Push the Sauté bottom and cook for about three minutes or until the clams are opaque and firm, then drizzle with thyme, salt, and black pepper. Stir to mix thoroughly.
6. Ladle the chowder in a big container and serve warm.

NUTRITIONAL INFO: calories: 252 ,total fat: 17.3g ,total carbs: 8.9g ,fiber: 2.1g ,net carbs: 6.8g ,protein: 17.1g

CAULIFLOWER, COCONUT MILK, AND SHRIMP SOUP

Time To Prepare: five minutes

Time to Cook: 2 hours and fifteen minutes

Yield: Servings 4

INGREDIENTS:

- 1 (13.5-ounce / 383-g) can unsweetened full-fat coconut milk
- 1 cup shrimp, peeled, deveined, tail off, and cooked
- 1 cup water
- 2 cups riced cauliflower
- 2 tablespoons chopped fresh cilantro leaves, divided
- 2 tablespoons red curry paste
- From the cupboard:

- Salt and freshly ground black pepper, to taste

DIRECTIONS:
1. Put in the riced cauliflower, red curry paste, coconut milk, 1 tablespoon cilantro, water, then drizzle with salt and black pepper. Combine the mixture to blend well.
2. Place the slow cooker lid on and cook on HIGH for about two hours.
3. Place the shrimp on a clean working surface, then drizzle salt and black pepper to season.
4. Place the shrimp in the slow cooker and cook for fifteen minutes more.
5. Move the soup into a big container and top with the rest of the cilantro leaves before you serve.

NUTRITIONAL INFO: calories: 268 ,total fat: 21.3g ,total carbs: 7.8g ,fiber: 3.2g ,net carbs: 4.6g ,protein: 16.1g

CELERY SOUP

Time To Prepare: ten minutes

Time to Cook: twenty minutes

Yield: Servings 4

INGREDIENTS:
- ½ cup brown onion, chopped
- ½ cup full-fat milk
- ½ pound with Salsiccia links, casing removed and cut
- ½ teaspoon dried chili flakes
- ½ teaspoon ground black pepper
- 1 carrot, chopped
- 1 garlic clove, pressed
- 2 teaspoon coconut oil
- 3 cups celery, chopped
- 3 cups roasted vegetable broth
- Kosher salt, to taste

DIRECTIONS:
1. Simply throw all of the above ingredients into your Instant Pot; gently stir until blended.
2. Secure the lid. Choose "Soup/Broth" mode and High pressure; cook for about twenty-five minutes. Once cooking is complete, use a quick pressure release; cautiously remove the lid.
3. Ladle into four soup bowls and serve hot. Enjoy!

NUTRITIONAL INFO: 150 Calories ,5.9g Fat ,5.9g Total Carbs ,16.4g Protein ,4.1g Sugars

CHEESY BROCCOLI SOUP

Time To Prepare: five minutes

Time to Cook: twenty minutes

Yield: Servings 4

INGREDIENTS:

- 1 cup broccoli, cut into florets
- 1 cup chicken broth
- 1 cup heavy whipping cream
- 1 cup shredded Cheddar cheese, plus more for topping
- 2 tablespoons butter
- From the cupboard:
- Salt and freshly ground black pepper, to taste

DIRECTIONS:

1. Place the butter in a deep cooking pan, and melt on moderate heat.
2. Put in and sauté the broccoli for four to five minutes or until tender.
3. Stir in the chicken broth and heavy whipping cream over the broccoli, and drizzle with salt and black pepper. Cook for approximately fifteen minutes or until the soup is smooth and thickened. Keep stirring during the cooking.
4. Lower the heat to low and gently fold in the Cheddar cheese. Keep stirring until well blended.
5. Ladle the soup into a big container. Spread more cheese over the soup before you serve.

NUTRITIONAL INFO: calories: 386 ,total fat: 37.3g ,total carbs: 3.8g ,fiber: 1.1g ,net carbs: 2.7g ,protein: 9.8g

CHEESY CHICKEN SOUP

Time To Prepare: twenty minutes

Time to Cook: 33-40 minutes

Yield: Servings 6

INGREDIENTS:

- ¼ teaspoon black pepper
- ½ cup shredded cheddar cheese
- ½ teaspoon cumin
- ½ teaspoon salt
- 1 cup whipped cream cheese
- 1 tablespoon coconut oil, for cooking
- 1 teaspoon chili powder
- 1 yellow onion, chopped
- 2 boneless, skinless chicken breasts
- 2 cloves garlic, chopped
- 2 cups chicken broth
- 2 cups water

DIRECTIONS:

1. Heat a big frying pan on moderate heat with a ½ tablespoon of the coconut oil.

2. Brown the chicken breasts until thoroughly cooked. Set aside.

3. Put in the garlic and onion to a big stockpot with the rest of the 1 tablespoon of the coconut oil and sauté until translucent over low to moderate heat. This should take about three to five minutes.

4. Put in this chicken broth and water.

5. Whisk in the cream cheese and keep whisking over low to moderate heat until blended.

6. Put in in the spices and bring to its boiling point.

7. While the water is boiling, chop the chicken into bite-sized pieces and put in to the stockpot.

8. Reduce to a simmer and cook for half an hour.

9. Mix in the cheddar cheese before you serve.

NUTRITIONAL INFO: Calories: 157 ,Carbohydrates: 5g ,Fiber: 1g Net ,Carbohydrates: 4g ,Fat: 7g ,Protein: 17g

CHEESY TOMATO AND BASIL SOUP

Time To Prepare: five minutes

Time to Cook: fifteen minutes

Yield: Servings 12

INGREDIENTS: ·

- ¼ teaspoon ground black pepper
- 1 tablespoon dried basil
- 1 teaspoon dried oregano
- 1 teaspoon salt
- 2 (14 ounces / 397 g) canned whole tomatoes, diced
- 2 garlic cloves, minced
- 2 tablespoons coconut oil
- 4 cups chicken broth
- 4 ounces (113 g) red onions, finely diced
- 5 ounces (142 g) grated Parmesan cheese, plus more for decoration
- 8 ounces (227 g) cream cheese, softened
- Fresh basil, chopped, for decoration

DIRECTIONS:

1. Grease a nonstick frying pan with coconut oil, and sauté the onions, basil, oregano, and garlic in the frying pan for about four minutes or until aromatic.

2. Put in the cream cheese and fully whisk until no clump, then fold in the chicken broth, and put in the cheese, tomatoes, salt, and pepper. Stir to blend well.

3. Cover the lid and bring them to a simmer on moderate heat for eight minutes. Move the soup into a blender, then blitz until it becomes thick.

4. Lightly pour the soup into a big serving container and sprinkle with Parmesan cheese and basil as decorate.

NUTRITIONAL INFO: calories: 146 ,total fat: 12g ,net carbs: 3g ,fiber: 1g ,protein: 6g

CHICKEN AND CAULIFLOWER CURRY STEW

Time To Prepare: fifteen minutes

Time to Cook: 4 hours

Yield: Servings 7

INGREDIENTS:

- ¼ cup fresh cilantro, chopped
- ⅓ cup coconut oil
- 1 green bell pepper, chopped
- 1 pound (454 g) cauliflower, chopped into little pieces
- 1.5pounds (680 g) skinless, boneless chicken thighs, cut into bite-sized pieces
- 14 ounces (397 g) unsweetened coconut milk
- 2 tablespoons curry powder
- 2 tablespoons ginger garlic paste
- Salt and ground black pepper, to taste

DIRECTIONS:

1. Warm half of the coconut oil in a nonstick frying pan on moderate heat, then sauté the garlic ginger paste and curry powder for a minutes or until aromatic.
2. Put in the chicken pieces, and drizzle with salt and pepper. sauté for another ten minutes or until the chicken is mildly browned. Remove from the frying pan and set aside in warm.
3. Warm another half of coconut oil in the frying pan, then sauté the cauliflower and bell pepper on moderate to high heat for one to two minutes.
4. Then fold in the coconut milk and reduce the heat to low. Cover with lid and stew for about forty-five minutes.
5. Drizzle with salt and pepper, then put in the sautéed chicken. Move the stew to a big platter and serve with cilantro on top as decorate.

NUTRITIONAL INFO: calories: 782 ,total fat: 68g ,net carbs: 9g ,fiber: 5g ,protein: 33g

CHICKEN AND KALE SOUP

Time To Prepare: five minutes

Time to Cook: 4 hours

Yield: Servings 4

INGREDIENTS:

- 1 (7-ounce / 198-g) bunch kale, trimmed and chopped
- 1 big chicken breast, cut into little strips
- 2 tablespoons olive oil

- 3 tablespoons fresh ginger, grated
- 6 cups chicken stock
- 6 garlic cloves, finely chopped
- From the cupboard:
- Salt and freshly ground black pepper, to taste

DIRECTIONS:
1. Grease the insert of the slow cooker with olive oil.
2. Combine the chicken breast, stock, kale, ginger, garlic, ginger, salt, and black pepper in the slow cooker.
3. Place the slow cooker lid on and cook on high for 4 hours.
4. Ladle the stew in a big container and serve warm.

NUTRITIONAL INFO: calories: 168 ,total fat: 7.6g ,total carbs: 8.3g ,fiber: 2.1g ,net carbs: 6.2g ,protein: 18.7g

CHICKEN CHILI BLANCO

Time To Prepare: ten minutes

Time to Cook: twenty minutes

Yield: Servings 4

INGREDIENTS:
- ¼ teaspoon cayenne pepper
- 1 tablespoon ghee
- 1 teaspoon chili powder
- 2 (4-ounce) cans diced mild green chiles with their liquid
- 2 scallions, cut
- 2 small onions, chopped
- 2 teaspoons dried oregano
- 4 cups chicken broth or vegetable broth
- 4 cups shredded cooked chicken
- 4 cups white beans, drained and washed well
- 4 teaspoons ground cumin
- 6 garlic cloves, minced

DIRECTIONS:
1. In a huge soup pot on moderate heat, melt the ghee.
2. Put in the onions and garlic, and sauté for five minutes.
3. Place the chiles, and cook for a couple of minutes, stirring.
4. Mix in the beans, broth, cumin, oregano, chili powder, and cayenne pepper. Heat it until it simmers.
5. Put in the chicken, bring to a simmer, decrease the heat to moderate-low, and cook for about ten minutes. Serve instantly, sprinkled with the scallions.

NUTRITIONAL INFO: Calories: 304 ,Total Fat: 4g ,Saturated Fat: 2g ,Cholesterol: 0mg ,Carbohydrates: 46g ,Fiber: 12g ,Protein: 21g

CHICKEN TORTILLA SOUP

Time To Prepare: ten minutes

Time to Cook: twenty minutes

Yield: Servings 8-10

INGREDIENTS:

- 1 teaspoon cayenne pepper or to taste
- 2 cups onions, chopped
- 2 teaspoons chili powder
- 2 teaspoons cumin powder
- 2 teaspoons dried oregano
- 2 teaspoons garlic powder
- 4 cups carrots, cut
- 4 cups celery, cut
- 4 cups water
- 4 teaspoons olive oil
- 6 cups rotisserie chicken, skinless, chopped or shredded
- 8 cloves garlic, minced
- 8 cups chicken broth
- 8 medium tomatoes, chopped
- Avocado, peeled, pitted, chopped
- For the topping: Use any (not necessary)
- Fresh cilantro, chopped
- Greek yogurt
- Pepper powder to taste
- Salt to taste
- Tortilla chips, crumbled

DIRECTIONS:

1. Put a soup pot on moderate heat. Put in oil.
2. When the oil is warmed, put the onion and celery and sauté until slightly soft.
3. Put in garlic and sauté for a few seconds until aromatic. Stir in the tomatoes and cook until tender. Remove the heat.
4. Move into a blender. Put in water and blend until the desired smoothness is achieved.
5. Put back the mixed mixture into the pot. Put in the remaining ingredients and stir.
6. If it's beginning to boil, reduce the heat then simmer until vegetables are tender.
7. Ladle into soup bowls before you serve.

NUTRITIONAL INFO: Calories: 1593 kcal ,Protein: 147.22 g ,Fat: 102.27 g ,Carbohydrates: 13.17 g

CHICKPEA CURRY SOUP

Time To Prepare: ten minutes

Time to Cook: twenty-five minutes

Yield: Servings 4

INGREDIENTS:

- ¼ cup extra-virgin olive oil or coconut oil
- 1 (fifteen-ounce) can chickpeas, drained and washed
- 1 big apple, cored, peeled, and slice into ¼-inch dice
- 1 cup full-fat coconut milk
- 1 medium onion, finely chopped
- 1 teaspoon salt
- 2 garlic cloves, cut
- 2 tablespoons finely chopped fresh cilantro
- 2 teaspoons curry powder
- 3 cups peeled butternut squash cut into ½-inch dice
- 3 cups vegetable broth

DIRECTIONS:

1. In a large pot, heat the oil on high heat.
2. Put in the onion and garlic and sauté until the onion starts to brown, six to eight minutes.
3. Place the apple, curry powder, and salt and sauté to toast the curry powder, one to two minutes.
4. Place the squash and broth then bring to its boiling point.
5. Reduce the heat then cook until the squash is soft about ten minutes.
6. Mix in the coconut milk.
7. Use an immersion blender to purée the soup in the pot until the desired smoothness is achieved.
8. Mix in the chickpeas and cilantro, heat through for one to two minutes, before you serve.

NUTRITIONAL INFO: Calories: 469 ,Total Fat: 30g ,Total Carbohydrates: 45g ,Sugar: 14g ,Fiber: 10g ,Protein: 12g ,Sodium: 1174mg

CLEAR CLAM CHOWDER

Time To Prepare: ten minutes

Time to Cook: fifteen minutes

Yield: Servings 4

INGREDIENTS:

- ¼ teaspoon freshly ground black pepper
- ½ teaspoon dried thyme
- ½ teaspoon salt
- 1 (10-ounce) can clams
- 1 (8-ounce) bottle clam juice
- 1 small red onion, cut into ¼-inch dice
- 2 celery stalks, thinly cut

- 2 cups vegetable broth
- 2 garlic cloves, cut
- 2 medium carrots, cut into ½-inch pieces
- 2 tablespoons unsalted butter

DIRECTIONS:

1. In a large pot, melt the butter on high heat.
2. Put in the carrots, celery, onion, and garlic and sauté until slightly softened two to three minutes.
3. Pour the broth and clam juice, then bring it to its boiling point.
4. Reduce the heat and cook until the carrots are soft, three to five minutes.
5. Mix in the clams and their juices, thyme, salt, and pepper, heat through for two to three minutes, before you serve.

NUTRITIONAL INFO: Calories: 156 ,Total Fat: 7g ,Total Carbohydrates: 7g ,Sugar: 3g ,Fiber: 1g ,Protein: 14g ,Sodium: 981mg

COCONUT CASHEW SOUP WITH BUTTERNUT SQUASH

Time To Prepare: ten minutes

Time to Cook: twenty minutes

Yield: Servings 6

INGREDIENTS:

- ½ tsp. salt
- ¾ cup toasted cashews
- 1 (14-ounce) can full-fat coconut milk
- 1 cup mung bean sprouts
- 1 small butternut squash, halved, diced
- 1 small Napa cabbage, shredded
- 1 white onion, diced
- 1½ tbsp. Ginger, peeled and minced
- 2 carrots, chopped
- 2 cups green beans, trimmed
- 2 red chili peppers, seeded and diced
- 2 tbsp. coconut oil
- 3 cups vegetable broth
- 3 garlic cloves, peeled and minced
- 4 tablespoons toasted coconut shavings
- Freshly ground black pepper

DIRECTIONS:

1. In a huge soup pot on moderate heat, melt the coconut oil.

2. Place the cashews and sauté for a couple of minutes. Take off from the pan and save for later.
3. Place the peppers, garlic, and onion, and sauté for minimum 6 minutes. Then put the ginger and carrots, and sauté for minimum 3 minutes, or until the carrots and squash start to become tender.
4. Stir in the cabbage, green beans, broth, coconut milk, and salt, flavor with pepper. Simmer for fifteen minutes. Remove the heat.
5. Mix in the bean sprouts and coconut shavings.
6. Pour into soup bowls and serve instantly.

NUTRITIONAL INFO: Calories: 340 ,Total Fat: 25g ,Saturated Fat: 20g ,Cholesterol: 0mg ,Carbohydrates: 23g ,Fiber: 5g ,Protein: 7g

COCONUT CURRIED BAN-APPLE SOUP

Time To Prepare: ten minutes

Time to Cook: 10-fifteen minutes

Yield: Servings 4

INGREDIENTS:
- ¼ cup toasted coconut, for decoration
- 1 big potato 1 Granny Smith apple
- 1 celery heart
- 1 cup coconut milk
- 1 ripe banana
- 1 sweet onion
- 1 teaspoon curry powder
- 1 teaspoon salt
- 2 cups Basic Vegetable Stock or low-sodium canned vegetable stock
- 2 tablespoons chopped fresh cilantro, for decoration

DIRECTIONS:
1. Place the vegetable stock in a soup pot.
2. Peel the banana and potato, cut them, and place them in the soup pot. Core the apple, cut it, and put in it to the soup pot. Cut the celery heart and onion and put in them to the soup pot.
3. Put the soup to its boiling point, then reduce the heat and simmer for ten to fifteen minutes. Put in the coconut milk, curry powder, and salt.
4. Place the hot soup in a blender and purée.
5. Serve the soup hot. Decorate using toasted coconut and cilantro.

NUTRITIONAL INFO: Calories: 344 ,Fat: 19 g ,Protein: 6 g ,Sodium: 886 mg ,Fiber: 7 g ,Carbohydrates: 40 g

CREAM OF MUSHROOM SOUP

Time To Prepare: twenty minutes

Time to Cook: thirty minutes

Yield: Servings 6

INGREDIENTS:

- 5 cups mushrooms (cut)
- 1 tablespoon sherry
- 3 tablespoons butter
- 3 tablespoons flour
- 1 cup half-and-half
- Salt
- Ground black pepper
- 1½ cups chicken broth
- ½ cup onion (chopped)
- 1/8 teaspoon dried thyme

DIRECTIONS:

1. Cook mushrooms with onion and thyme in the broth until soft.
2. Puree the mixture.
3. Whisk some flour in a pan of melted butter. Put in half-and-half, vegetable puree, and seasoning. Boil until it becomes thick.
4. Put in sherry.

NUTRITIONAL INFO: Calories: 148 kcal ,Carbohydrates: 8.6 g ,Fat: 11 g ,Protein: 4 g

CREAMY & CULTURE TOMATO SAUCE

Time To Prepare: ten minutes

Time to Cook: fifteen-twenty minutes

Yield: Servings 6

INGREDIENTS:

- ⅛ teaspoon dried thyme
- ⅛ teaspoon freshly ground black pepper
- ¼ cup tomato paste
- ¼ teaspoon chili powder
- ½ cup plain whole-milk yogurt
- ½ teaspoon salt
- 1 small onion, chopped
- 1 tablespoon ghee
- 1 teaspoon dried basil
- 1 teaspoon dried oregano
- 2 (14-ounce) cans diced tomatoes with their juice
- 2 cups vegetable broth
- 3 garlic cloves, chopped

DIRECTIONS:

1. In a huge soup pot on moderate heat, melt the ghee.
2. Place the onion and garlic, and sauté for five minutes.
3. Stir in the basil, oregano, salt, chili powder, pepper, and thyme.
4. Place the tomatoes, broth, and tomato paste, and stir until blended. Heat to a simmer, turn the heat to low, and cook for five to ten minutes. Take away the pot from the heat. With an immersion blender (or in batches in a standard blender), purée the mixture in the pot until you have the desired consistency.
5. Put in the yogurt. Blend for a minute more. Serve instantly.

NUTRITIONAL INFO: Calories: 157 ,Total Fat: 6g ,Saturated Fat: 3g ,Cholesterol: 3mg ,Carbohydrates: 25g ,Fiber: 13g ,Protein: 8g

CREAMY BROCCOLI SOUP

Time To Prepare: fifteen minutes

Time to Cook: 4 hours

Yield: Servings 7

INGREDIENTS:

- ¼ teaspoon ground black pepper
- ½ teaspoon paprika powder
- ½ teaspoon salt
- ⅔ cup heavy whipping cream
- 1 pinch cayenne pepper
- 1 red onion, roughly chopped
- 1 tablespoon olive oil
- 2 cups chicken broth
- 20 ounces (567 g) broccoli, cut into stalks and florets
- 3 garlic cloves, chopped
- 3 tablespoons butter
- ounces (99 g) Cheddar cheese, shredded

DIRECTIONS:

1. Warm 1 tablespoon of butter and olive oil in a deep cooking pan, then fry the broccoli stalks and chopped onion on moderate heat for five minutes until soft.
2. Put in the garlic and keep frying for a couple of minutes until mildly browned, then drizzle with cayenne pepper, paprika, salt, and ground black pepper. Cook for another one minutes.
3. Pour over the chicken broth. Cover the lid and leave to simmer for five minutes.
4. Take away the cooked vegetables from the deep cooking pan to a food processor and process. Lightly ladle the soup into the food processor while processing until creamy.
5. Melt the rest of the butter in the deep cooking pan, and fry the broccoli florets for five minutes until tender and soft.
6. Pour the soup from the food processor into the deep cooking pan. Blend to mix thoroughly. If the soup is too thick, you can put in some water to make it thinner.

7. Bring the soup to its boiling point, then reduce the heat and bring to a simmer using low heat for about three minutes.
8. Put in the Cheddar cheese and heavy whipping cream and cook for a couple of minutes more until the cheese melts.
9. Take away the soup from the deep cooking pan and serve warm.

NUTRITIONAL INFO: calories: 266 ,total fat: 23g ,net carbs: 7g ,fiber: 3g ,protein: 8g

CREAMY CELERY AND CHICKEN BROTH

Time To Prepare: five minutes

Time to Cook: twenty minutes

Yield: Servings 4

INGREDIENTS:
- ¼ cup celery, chopped
- ½ cup coconut cream
- 1 onion, chopped
- 2 chicken breasts, chopped
- 3 tablespoons butter
- 4 cups water
- From The Cupboard:
- Salt and freshly ground black pepper, to taste

DIRECTIONS:

1. Place the butter in a deep cooking pan, and melt on moderate heat.
2. Put in and sauté the celery and onion for about three minutes or until the onion is translucent.
3. Put in the chicken, salt, black pepper, and water, and simmer for fifteen minutes. Keep stirring during the simmering.
4. Mix in the coconut cream. Pour the soup in a big container and serve warm.

NUTRITIONAL INFO: calories: 398 ,total fat: 24.4g ,net carbs: 5.9g ,protein: 29.3g

CREAMY LEEK SOUP

Time To Prepare: two minutes

Time to Cook: 8 minutes

Yield: Servings 4

INGREDIENTS:
- ½ cup heavy cream
- ½ cup Monterey-Jack cheese, shredded
- ½ cup tomato purée
- ½ pound chorizo, cut

- 1 bay leaf
- 1 cup leeks, chopped
- 1 green chili, deseeded and finely chopped
- 1 tablespoon sesame oil
- 2 chicken bouillon cubes
- 2 cloves garlic, minced
- 4 cups water

DIRECTIONS:

1. Push the "Sauté" button to heat up your Instant Pot. Once hot, heat the oil and sauté the leeks until soft.
2. Now, mix in chorizo, garlic, and green chili; carry on cooking until aromatic. Next, put in water, tomato puree, heavy cream, bouillon cubes, and bay leaf.
3. Secure the lid. Choose "Manual" mode and High pressure; cook for about six minutes. Once cooking is complete, use a natural pressure release; cautiously remove the lid.
4. Next, press the "Sauté" button and put in the cheese; allow it to simmer until the cheese is melted and thoroughly heated.

NUTRITIONAL INFO: 428 Calories ,36g Fat ,6.1g Total Carbs ,18.9g Protein ,2.1g Sugars

CREAMY PARSNIP SOUP

Time To Prepare: twenty-five minutes

Time to Cook: 60 minutes

Yield: Servings 10

INGREDIENTS:

- 1 big onion (diced)
- 1 cup whole milk
- 1 tablespoon brown sugar
- 1 tablespoon butter
- 1 tablespoon olive oil
- 1 teaspoon ground ginger
- ½ teaspoon ground allspice
- ½ teaspoon ground cardamom
- ½ teaspoon ground nutmeg
- 1/4 teaspoon cayenne pepper
- 2 pounds parsnips (peeled, cut)
- 3 carrots (peeled, cut)
- 3 cloves garlic (minced)
- 3 stalks celery (diced)
- 4 cups chicken stock
- Ground black pepper
- Salt

DIRECTIONS:

1. Preheat your oven to 425 F.
2. Toss the parsnips and carrots with oil and seasoning in a container. Put them over a baking sheet.
3. Roast in oven until for half an hour
4. Cook the onion and celery in oil till golden brown, approximately seven minutes. Put in butter, brown sugar, garlic, and the parsnips and carrots, cooking for about ten minutes.
5. Season and stir. Put in the chicken stock to its boiling point until soft.
6. Puree the soup.
7. Put in milk and cream and simmer some more before you serve with seasoning.

NUTRITIONAL INFO: Calories: 187 kcal ,Carbohydrates: 24 g ,Fat: 9 g ,Protein: 3 g

CREAMY PUMPKIN PUREE SOUP

Time To Prepare: ten minutes

Time to Cook: forty-five minutes

Yield: Servings 3

INGREDIENTS:

*   1 cup Heavy Cream
*   1 cup Pumpkin puree
*   2 cups Chicken broth
*   2 tbsp. Olive oil
*   4-5 Garlic cloves
*   Salt and black pepper to taste

DIRECTIONS:

1. In the Instant Pot, put in all ingredients.
2. Secure the lid and cook for forty minutes on Meat/Stew mode on High. When ready, press Cancel and do a quick pressure release.
3. Move to a blender and blend thoroughly. Pour into serving bowls to serve.

NUTRITIONAL INFO: Calories 465 ,Protein: 15.4g ,Carbs: 6.2g ,Fat: 43.5g

CREAMY TURKEY SOUP

Time To Prepare: fifteen minutes

Time to Cook: 4 hours

Yield: Servings 7

INGREDIENTS:

*   1 carrot, chopped
*   1 cup cream cheese
*   1 pound turkey breast, cubed

- 1 stalk celery, chopped
- 1 teaspoon freshly chopped rosemary
- 3 cloves garlic, chopped
- 5 cups chicken broth
- Salt & black pepper, to taste

DIRECTIONS:

1. Put in all the ingredients minus the cream cheese to the base of a slow cooker.
2. Cook on high for 4 hours.
3. Mix in the cream cheese until well blended.

NUTRITIONAL INFO: Calories: 216 ,Carbohydrates: 6g ,Fiber: 1g Net ,Carbohydrates: 5g ,Fat: 14g ,Protein: 17g

CREAMY TURMERIC CAULIFLOWER SOUP

Time To Prepare: ten minutes

Time to Cook: fifteen minutes

Yield: Servings 4

INGREDIENTS:

- ¼ cup finely chopped fresh cilantro
- ¼ teaspoon freshly ground black pepper
- ¼ teaspoon ground cumin
- ½ teaspoon salt
- 1 (1¼-inch) piece fresh ginger, peeled and cut
- 1 cup full-fat coconut milk
- 1 garlic clove, peeled
- 1 leek, white part only, thinly cut
- 1½ teaspoons turmeric
- 2 tablespoons extra-virgin olive oil
- 3 cups cauliflower florets
- 3 cups vegetable broth

DIRECTIONS:

1. In a large pot, heat the oil on high heat.
2. Put in the leek, and sauté until it just starts to brown, three to four minutes.
3. Put in the cauliflower, garlic, ginger, turmeric, salt, pepper, and cumin and sauté to lightly toast the spices, one to two minutes.
4. Pour the broth then bring to its boiling point.
5. Reduce the heat and cook until the cauliflower is soft about five minutes.
6. Use an immersion blender to purée the soup in the pot until the desired smoothness is achieved.

7. Stir in the coconut milk and cilantro, heat through, before you serve.

NUTRITIONAL INFO: Calories: 264 ,Total Fat: 23g ,Total Carbohydrates: 12g ,Sugar: 5g ,Fiber: 4g ,Protein: 7g ,Sodium: 900mg

CROCK-POT TURKEY TACO SOUP

Time To Prepare: ten minutes

Time to Cook: 4 hours

Yield: Servings 6

INGREDIENTS:

- 1 cup canned diced tomatoes (no sugar added)
- 1 cup whipped cream cheese
- 1 pound ground turkey
- 1 tablespoon chili powder
- 1 teaspoon cumin
- 1 teaspoon garlic powder
- 1 teaspoon onion powder
- 1 yellow onion, chopped
- 5 cups chicken bone broth (you can also use regular chicken broth)

DIRECTIONS:

1. Put in all the ingredients to the base of a Crock-Pot minus the cream cheese and cover with the chicken broth.
2. Set on high and cook for 4 hours putting in in the cream cheese at the 3.5 hour mark.
3. Stir thoroughly before you serve.

NUTRITIONAL INFO: Calories: 335,Carbohydrates: 6g,Fiber: 1gNet ,Carbohydrates: 5g,Fat: 23g,Protein: 28g

DETOX CABBAGE SOUP

Time To Prepare: ten minutes

Time to Cook: thirty-five minutes

Yield: Servings 4

INGREDIENTS:

- 1 tbs. freshly grated ginger root
- 2 big carrot
- 1 cup whole canned tomatoes with juice
- 1 whole head of cabbage
- 1 tbs. freshly grated turmeric root
- 3 celery stalks with leaves

- Enough water to immerse the vegetables
- 2 medium Russet potatoes
- Sea salt & black pepper to taste
- ½ medium onion
- 1/4 cup extra virgin olive oil

DIRECTIONS:

1. Heat the oil in a large pot on moderate heat for a couple of minutes.
2. Put in the celery, onions, ginger, carrots & turmeric, then sauté on medium until translucent. Sprinkle with salt & pepper to taste.
3. With the heat still on moderate, dice the potatoes & generally slash the cabbage at that point put in to the pot alongside the whole tomatoes & juice.
4. While they cook, break separated the tomatoes using a fork or blade. Fill the pot with sufficient water to simply cover the cabbage.
5. Cover with a top & heat to the point of boiling. When bubbling, evacuate the top & cook for around thirty minutes or until the potatoes & cabbage are fork delicate. Put in the ice chest for as long as 5 days & in the cooler for as long as three months.

NUTRITIONAL INFO: Calories: 359 kcal ,Protein: 10.85 g ,Fat: 12.68 g ,Carbohydrates: 54.94 g

FENNEL AND PEAR SOUP

Time To Prepare: fifteen minutes

Time to Cook: twenty minutes

Yield: Servings 4

INGREDIENTS:

- ⅛ Teaspoon ground nutmeg
- ¼ cup freshly squeezed lemon juice
- ¼ cup honey
- ¼ teaspoon freshly ground black pepper
- 1 teaspoon finely chopped fresh tarragon
- 1 teaspoon salt
- 2 fennel bulbs, trimmed and slice into ½-inch dice
- 2 shallots, halved
- 2 tablespoons extra-virgin olive oil
- 4 cups vegetable broth
- 4 pears, cored and slice into ½-inch dice

DIRECTIONS:

1. In a large pot, heat the oil on high heat.
2. Put in the pears, fennel, and shallots, and sauté until the pears and fennel barely start to brown, approximately five minutes.
3. Pour the broth, then bring to its boiling point.
4. Reduce the heat to a simmer, then cook, once in a while stirring, until the fennel is soft, 5 to 8 minutes.

5. Stir in the lemon juice, honey, salt, pepper, and nutmeg.
6. Use an immersion blender to purée the soup in the pot until the desired smoothness is achieved.
7. Drizzle with the tarragon before you serve.

NUTRITIONAL INFO: Calories: 328 ,Total Fat: 9g ,Total Carbohydrates: 60g ,Sugar: 39g ,Fiber: 10g ,Protein: 7g ,Sodium: 1413mg

FRENCH CARAMELIZED ONION SOUP

Time To Prepare: five minutes

Time to Cook: ten minutes

Yield: Servings 4

INGREDIENTS:
- ½ stick butter, softened
- 4 cups chicken stock
- ½ teaspoon dried basil
- Kosher salt and ground black pepper, to taste
- ½ cup Swiss cheese, freshly grated
- 3/4 pound yellow onions, cut

DIRECTIONS:
1. Push the "Sauté" button to heat up your Instant Pot. Once hot, melt the butter and sauté the onions until caramelized and soft.
2. Put in chicken stock, basil, salt, and black pepper.
3. Secure the lid. Choose "Manual" mode and High pressure; cook for about ten minutes. Once cooking is complete, use a quick pressure release; cautiously remove the lid.
4. Ladle the soup into separate bowls and top with grated cheese. Enjoy!

NUTRITIONAL INFO: 228 Calories ,18g Fat ,5.3g Total Carbs ,10.5g Protein ,3.5g Sugars

GARLIC AND LENTIL SOUP

Time To Prepare: fifteen minutes

Time to Cook: fifteen minutes

Yield: Servings 4

INGREDIENTS:
- ¼ cup chopped walnuts (not necessary)
- ¼ teaspoon freshly ground black pepper
- 1 (fifteen-ounce) can lentils, drained and washed
- 1 small white onion, cut into ¼-inch dice
- 1 tablespoon minced or grated orange zest
- 1 teaspoon ground cinnamon

- 1 teaspoon salt
- 2 garlic cloves, thinly cut
- 2 medium carrots, thinly cut
- 2 tablespoons extra-virgin olive oil
- 2 tablespoons finely chopped fresh flat-leaf parsley
- 3 cups vegetable broth

DIRECTIONS:

1. In a large pot, heat the oil using high heat.
2. Put in the carrots, onion, and garlic and sauté until tender, five to seven minutes.
3. Place the cinnamon, salt, and pepper and stir to uniformly coat the vegetables, one to two minutes.
4. Pour the broth then bring to its boiling point.
5. Reduce the heat to a simmer, put in the lentils and cook until they are thoroughly heated about one minute.
6. Mix in the orange zest and serve, sprinkled with the walnuts (if using) and parsley.

NUTRITIONAL INFO: Calories: 201 ,Total Fat: 8g ,Total Carbohydrates 22g ,Sugar: 4g ,Fiber: 8g ,Protein: 11g ,Sodium: 1178mg

GARLIC MUSHROOM & BEEF SOUP

Time To Prepare: ten minutes

Time to Cook: forty minutes

Yield: Servings 6

INGREDIENTS:

- ½ cup heavy cream
- ½ cup whipped cream cheese
- 1 pound beef chuck, cubed
- 1 tablespoon coconut oil, for cooking
- 1 yellow onion, chopped
- 1½ cups cremini mushrooms
- 2 cloves garlic, chopped
- 6 cups beef broth
- Salt & pepper, to taste

DIRECTIONS:

1. Put in the coconut oil to a frying pan and brown the beef.
2. Once cooked, put in the beef to the base of a stockpot with all of the ingredients minus the heavy cream. Mix thoroughly.
3. Heat to a simmer and whisk again until the cream cheese is mixed uniformly into the soup.
4. Cook for half an hour
5. Warm the heavy cream, and then put in to the soup.

NUTRITIONAL INFO: Calories: 315,Carbohydrates: 5g,Fiber: 1gNet ,Carbohydrates: 4g,Fat: 19g,Protein: 30g

GARLICKY CHICKEN SOUP

Time To Prepare: ten minutes

Time to Cook: fifteen minutes

Yield: Servings 6

INGREDIENTS:

- ¼ teaspoon black pepper
- ½ cup whipped cream cheese
- 1 tablespoon butter for cooking
- 1 teaspoon salt
- 1 teaspoon thyme
- 2 boneless, skinless chicken breasts
- 3 cloves garlic, chopped
- 4 cups chicken broth

DIRECTIONS:

1. Preheat a stockpot on moderate heat with the butter.
2. Put in the chicken and brown until completely thoroughly cooked. Turn off the heat.
3. Shred the chicken and put in it back to the stockpot together with the rest of the ingredients minus the cream cheese.
4. Heat to a simmer.
5. Put in in the cream cheese and whisk until there are no more clumps.
6. Simmer for about ten minutes before you serve.

NUTRITIONAL INFO: Calories: 128 ,Carbohydrates: 2g ,Fiber: 0g Net ,Carbohydrates: 2g ,Fat: 6g ,Protein: 16g

GOLDEN CHICKPEA AND VEGETABLE SOUP

Time To Prepare: fifteen minutes

Time to Cook: twenty minutes

Yield: Servings 6

INGREDIENTS:

- 1 ½ cup Diced celery
- 1 ½ cup Sliced leeks
- 1 cup cooked chickpeas

- 1 cup diced carrots
- 1 cup Torn curly kale leaves
- 1 tbsp. Grated ginger
- 2 cloves minced garlic
- 2 cups Cauliflower florets
- 2 tbsp. Curry powder
- 2 tbsp. Minced organic parsley
- 2 tsp. Coconut oil
- 4 cups Bone broth

DIRECTIONS:

1. Warm the coconut oil in a pot and put in the garlic and ginger. Sauté for one minute before you put in the turmeric and curry powder and sautéing for one more minute.
2. Throw in celery, leeks, carrots, and cauliflower, continuously stirring for approximately one minute.
3. Put in the bone broth and chickpeas. Cover the pot and leave to boil. Reduce the heat and allow it to simmer for minimum fifteen minutes.
4. Turn off heat and put in parsley and kale, leaving the heat to cook the leaves.
5. Drizzle salt and pepper.
6. Serve.

NUTRITIONAL INFO: Calories: 142 kcal ,Protein: 8.64 g ,Fat: 4.79 g ,Carbohydrates: 17.57 g

GREEK SPLIT PEA SOUP

Time To Prepare: fifteen minutes

Time to Cook: 2 hours

Yield: Servings 6

INGREDIENTS:

- 1 pinch dried marjoram
- 1 potato (diced)
- 1½ pounds ham bone
- 2 onions (cut)
- 2 quarts cold water
- 2-1/4 cups dried split peas
- 3 carrots, (chopped)
- 3 stalks celery (chopped)
- Ground black pepper
- Salt

DIRECTIONS:

1. Simmer the peas in a pot for a couple of minutes and then soak for an hour.
2. Put in ham bone, onion, marjoram, and seasoning.
3. Boil for 1½hours.

4. Remove bone and meat. Put in the meat (diced) to the soup.
5. Put the rest of the vegetables and cook until soft.

NUTRITIONAL INFO: Calories: 310 kcal ,Carbohydrates: 58 g ,Fat: 20 g ,Protein: 2 g

GREEN BLAST SOUP

Time To Prepare: ten minutes

Time to Cook: twenty minutes

Yield: Servings 4

INGREDIENTS:

- ¼ cup chopped cashews (not necessary)
- ¼ cup extra-virgin olive oil
- ¼ teaspoon freshly ground black pepper
- 1 bunch Swiss chard, crudely chopped
- 1 fennel bulb, trimmed and thinly cut
- 1 garlic clove, peeled
- 1 teaspoon salt
- 2 leeks, white parts only, thinly cut
- 2 tablespoons apple cider vinegar
- 3 cups vegetable broth
- 4 cups crudely chopped kale
- 4 cups crudely chopped mustard greens

DIRECTIONS:

1. In a large pot, heat the oil on high heat.
2. Put in the leeks, fennel, and garlic and sauté until tender, for approximately five minutes.
3. Put in the Swiss chard, kale, and mustard greens and sauté until the greens wilt, two to three minutes.
4. Pour the broth then bring to its boiling point.
5. Reduce the heat to a simmer and cook until the vegetables are completely tender and soft about five minutes.
6. Mix in the vinegar, salt, pepper, and cashews (if using).
7. Use an immersion blender to purée the soup in the pot until the desired smoothness is achieved before you serve.

NUTRITIONAL INFO: Calories: 238 ,Total Fat: 14g ,Total Carbohydrates: 22g ,Sugar: 4g ,Fiber: 6g ,Protein: 9g ,Sodium: 1294mg

GUT-HEALING BONE BROTH

Time To Prepare: fifteen minutes

Time to Cook: 8 to one day

Yield: Servings 4

INGREDIENTS:

- 1 medium onion, chopped
- 1 tablespoon apple cider vinegar
- 2 bay leaves
- 2 celery stalks, chopped
- 2 pounds beef marrow bones
- 3 medium carrots, chopped
- 4 garlic cloves
- Filtered water, to cover

DIRECTIONS:

1. In a 6-quart slow cooker, mix the bones, garlic, carrots, celery, onion, bay leaves, and vinegar. Cover with filtered water. Set the cooker on low and simmer for minimum 8 hours and up to one day.
2. Skim off and discard any foam that forms on the surface. Ladle the broth through a fine-mesh sieve or cheesecloth to strain out the solids. Pour into airtight glass containers. The broth can be placed in the fridge for maximum one week; just boil it again before use. To freeze, let the broth fully cool and then fill jars up to an inch below the top to allow for expansion, and keep for four to 5 months.

NUTRITIONAL INFO: Calories: 40 ,Total Fat: 0g ,Saturated Fat: 0g ,Cholesterol: 0mg ,Carbohydrates: 5g ,Fiber: 0g ,Protein: 6g

HAMBURGER & TOMATO SOUP

Time To Prepare: ten minutes

Time to Cook: 4 hours

Yield: Servings 6

INGREDIENTS:

- ½ cup beef broth
- ½ cup no-sugar added marinara sauce
- ½ cup shredded cheddar cheese
- 1 pound lean ground beef
- 1 yellow onion, chopped
- 2 cloves garlic, chopped
- Salt & pepper, to taste

DIRECTIONS:

1. Put in all the ingredients to a slow cooker minus the shredded cheese and cook on high for 4 hours.
2. Mix in the cheese before you serve.

NUTRITIONAL INFO: Calories: 209 ,Carbohydrates: 5g ,Fiber: 1g Net ,Carbohydrates: 4g ,Fat: 9g ,Protein: 26g

HARVEST STEW

Time To Prepare: fifteen minutes

Time to Cook: 60 minutes

Yield: Servings 6

INGREDIENTS:

- ¼ cup flour
- ½ cup cut carrots
- ½ cup diced celery
- ¾ cup diced onions
- 1 bay leaf
- 1 leek, cleaned and diced
- 1 potato, peeled and diced
- 1 pound stewing beef cubes
- 2 cups diced zucchini
- 2 tablespoons olive oil
- 2 tablespoons Worcestershire sauce
- 2 tomatoes, chopped
- 3 sprigs fresh thyme
- 3 turnips, diced
- 4 cups low-sodium beef broth
- 6 garlic cloves, peeled
- Salt and pepper, to taste

DIRECTIONS:

1. Brown the beef cubes in olive oil. Dust the flour on the meat and stir to coat and spread.
2. Put in the onions, carrots, celery, leek, garlic, zucchini, potato, turnips, tomatoes, bay leaf, thyme sprigs, and beef broth. Put to its boiling point, then reduce the heat and simmer for 60 minutes.
3. Take away the bay leaf and thyme sprigs. Put in the Worcestershire sauce, salt, and pepper. Serve hot.

NUTRITIONAL INFO: Calories: 254 ,Fat: 9.5 g ,Protein: 20 g ,Sodium: 514 mg ,Fiber: 3.5 g ,Carbohydrates: 22 g

HEARTY ROOT VEGETABLE SOUP

Time To Prepare: five minutes

Time to Cook: ten minutes

Yield: Servings 4

INGREDIENTS:

- 1 bay leaf
- 1 carrot, cut

- 1 celery, diced
- 1 garlic clove, minced
- 1 parsnip, cut
- 1 tablespoon fresh parsley, roughly chopped
- 1 teaspoon fresh sage
- 2 cups cauliflower, cut into little florets
- 4 cups chicken stock
- 4 tablespoons olive oil
- Kosher salt and freshly ground black pepper, to taste

DIRECTIONS:

1. Simply drop all of the above ingredients into your Instant Pot.
2. Secure the lid. Choose "Manual" mode and High pressure; cook for about ten minutes. Once cooking is complete, use a natural pressure release; cautiously remove the lid.
3. Taste, calibrate the seasonings and serve instantly. Enjoy!

NUTRITIONAL INFO: 190 Calories ,15.6g Fat ,6.1g Total Carbs ,6.7g Protein ,2.6g Sugars

HUNGARIAN LENTIL SOUP

Time To Prepare: fifteen minutes

Time to Cook: 2 hours

Yield: Servings 8

INGREDIENTS:

- 7 Cups Chicken Stock
- 3 Carrots (Diced)
- 2 Stalks Celery (Diced)
- 1 Teaspoon Garlic (Minced)
- 2 Bay Leaves
- 1 Sprig Fresh Parsley (Chopped)
- 2 Tablespoons Olive Oil
- 2 Large Onions (Cubed)
- Salt
- Ground Black Pepper
- 1½ Cups Lentils (Soaked, Rinsed, Drained)
- ½ Teaspoon Paprika
- ½ Cup Grated Parmesan Cheese
- 3½ Cups Crushed Tomatoes
- 3/4 Cup White Wine

DIRECTIONS:

1. Sauté onions in oil until shiny and put in garlic, paprika, celery, and carrots, cooking for about ten minutes.

2. Mix in tomatoes, chicken stock, lentils, bay leaves, seasoning, and wine to boil.
3. Cook until the lentils are soft.
4. Top with parsley and Parmesan before you serve.

NUTRITIONAL INFO: Calories: 258 kcal ,Carbohydrates: 34 g ,Fat: 6 g ,Protein: 14 g

ITALIAN BEEF SOUP

Time To Prepare: ten minutes

Time to Cook: 4 hours

Yield: Servings 6

INGREDIENTS:

- ½ cup diced tomatoes
- ½ cup shredded mozzarella cheese
- 1 cup beef broth
- 1 cup heavy cream
- 1 pound lean ground beef
- 1 tablespoon Italian seasoning
- 1 yellow onion, chopped
- 2 cloves garlic, chopped
- Salt & pepper, to taste

DIRECTIONS:

1. Put in all the ingredients to a slow cooker minus the heavy cream and mozzarella cheese. Cook on high for 4 hours.
2. Warm the heavy cream, and then put in the warmed cream and cheese to the soup. Stir thoroughly before you serve.

NUTRITIONAL INFO: Calories: 241 ,Carbohydrates: 4g ,Fiber: 1g Net ,Carbohydrates: 3g ,Fat: 14g ,Protein: 25g

ITALIAN MODENA SOUP

Time To Prepare: two minutes

Time to Cook: 8 minutes

Yield: Servings 4

INGREDIENTS:

- ½ cup Parmigiano-Reggiano cheese, shaved
- ½ teaspoon crushed chili
- 1 cup water
- 1 onion, chopped
- 1 tablespoon Italian seasonings

- 16 ounces Cotechino di Modena, cut
- 2 cups tomatoes, purée
- 2 tablespoons olive oil
- 3 cups roasted vegetable broth
- Sea salt and ground black pepper, to taste

DIRECTIONS:

1. Push the "Sauté" button to heat up your Instant Pot. Once hot, heat the oil and sauté the onions until soft and translucent.
2. Now, put in the sausage and cook an additional three minutes,
3. Mix in tomatoes, broth, water, sea salt, black pepper, crushed chili, and Italian seasonings.
4. Secure the lid. Choose "Manual" mode and High pressure; cook for five minutes. Once cooking is complete, use a quick pressure release; cautiously remove the lid.
5. Top with shaved Parmigiano-Reggiano cheese and serve warm

NUTRITIONAL INFO: 340 Calories ,27.9g Fat ,5g Total Carbs ,14.1g Protein ,2.6g Sugars

ITALIAN SUMMER SQUASH SOUP

Time To Prepare: ten minutes

Time to Cook: fifteen minutes

Yield: Servings 4

INGREDIENTS:

- ½ cup shredded carrot
- 1 cup shredded yellow squash
- 1 cup shredded zucchini
- 1 garlic clove, minced
- 1 small red onion, thinly cut
- 1 tablespoon finely chopped fresh chives
- 1 teaspoon salt
- 2 tablespoons finely chopped fresh basil
- 2 tablespoons pine nuts
- 3 cups vegetable broth
- 3 tablespoons extra-virgin olive oil

DIRECTIONS:

1. In a large pot, heat the oil using high heat.
2. Put in the onion and garlic and sauté until tender, five to seven minutes.
3. Put in the zucchini, yellow squash, and carrot and sauté until tender, one to two minutes.
4. Pour the broth and salt then bring to its boiling point.
5. Reduce the heat and cook until the vegetables are soft, one to two minutes.
6. Mix in the basil and chives and serve, sprinkled with the pine nuts.

NUTRITIONAL INFO: Calories: 172 ,Total Fat: 15g ,Total Carbohydrates: 6g ,Sugar: 3g ,Fiber: 2g ,Protein: 5g ,Sodium: 1170mg

KUMARA & CHICKPEA SOUP

Time To Prepare: twenty-five minutes

Time to Cook: thirty-five minutes

Yield: Servings 6

INGREDIENTS:

- 1 bay leaf
- 1 onion (chopped)
- 1 teaspoon dried basil
- 1 tomato (chopped)
- ½ teaspoon dried thyme
- 1/4 teaspoon paprika
- 2 cloves garlic (minced)
- 2 cups kumara (peeled, chopped)
- 2 tablespoons olive oil
- 200g garbanzo beans
- 3 cups chicken broth
- Ground black pepper
- Mixed vegetables
- Salt

DIRECTIONS:

1. Sauté onion, garlic, and sweet potatoes in oil for five minutes.
2. Put in broth, bay leaf, herbs, and seasoning.
3. Boil until soft.
4. Put in tomato, beans, and chickpeas, simmering some more before you serve.

NUTRITIONAL INFO: Calories: 197 kcal ,Carbohydrates: 30 g ,Fat: 6 g ,Protein: 7.5 g

LAMB STEW

Time To Prepare: five minutes

Time to Cook: 8 hours

Yield: Servings 6

INGREDIENTS:

- 1 lamb stock cube
- 1 onion, roughly chopped
- 2 pounds (907 g) boneless lamb, cut into cubes

- 2 tablespoons olive oil, plus more for greasing the frying pan
- 2 teaspoons dried rosemary
- 3 cups water
- 4 garlic cloves, finely chopped
- From the cupboard:
- Salt and freshly ground black pepper, to taste

DIRECTIONS:

1. Position the lamb into a mildly greased nonstick frying pan, and cook using high heat for a couple of minutes or until browned.
2. Grease a slow cooker with olive oil, then put in the cooked lamb, stock cube, rosemary, onion, garlic, salt, black pepper, and 3 cups of water. Blend to blend well.
3. Place the slow cooker lid on and cook on LOW for eight hours.
4. Take away the cooked lamb stew from the slow cooker and serve warm.

NUTRITIONAL INFO: calories: 252 ,total fat: 9.5g ,carbs: 4.9g ,protein: 34.9g

LAMB TACO SOUP

Time To Prepare: ten minutes

Time to Cook: 4-6 hours minutes

Yield: Servings 6

INGREDIENTS:

- ½ teaspoon cayenne pepper
- 1 cup diced tomatoes
- 1 cup shredded cheddar cheese
- 1 green bell pepper, chopped
- 1 pound ground lamb
- 1 teaspoon ground coriander
- 1 teaspoon ground cumin
- 1 teaspoon paprika
- 1 yellow onion, chopped
- 2 cloves garlic, chopped
- 4 cups beef broth
- Salt & pepper, to taste

DIRECTIONS:

1. Put in all the ingredients to a slow cooker minus the shredded cheese and cook on high for four to 6 hours.
2. Mix in the shredded cheese before you serve.

NUTRITIONAL INFO: Calories: 265 ,Carbohydrates: 6g ,Fiber: 1g Net ,Carbohydrates: 5g ,Fat: 13g ,Protein: 30g

LEBANESE LENTIL SOUP

Time To Prepare: fifteen minutes

Time to Cook: 60 minutes

Yield: Servings 6

INGREDIENTS:
- 1 cup brown lentils
- 1 lemon juiced
- 1 medium onion
- 1 tablespoon olive oil
- 2 medium carrots
- 2 teaspoons cinnamon
- 2 teaspoons cumin
- 3 stalks celery
- 4 cloves garlic
- 4 cups chicken broth low sodium
- 4 cups water
- 8 cups spinach
- salt& pepper to taste

DIRECTIONS:
1. Over moderate heat, heat oil in a soup pot, Put in & cook carrots, celery & onions until become soft for seven minutes, put in pepper & salt to taste.
2. Stir cumin, cinnamon & garlic heat it for 30-60 minutes. Put in lentils & heat for a couple of minutes to slightly toast. Pour in the lemon juice, water & chicken broth, then bring the pot to its boiling point. When lentils are soft, decrease the heat to low & simmer, approximately 30-45 minutes.
3. Before you serve, mix in the spinach, cook until the color is green, now served to put in pepper, lemon juice & salt.

NUTRITIONAL INFO: Calories: 102 kcal ,Protein: 6.33 g ,Fat: 4.58 g ,Carbohydrates: 11.6 g

LEEK, CHICKEN AND SPINACH SOUP

Time To Prepare: ten minutes

Time to Cook: fifteen minutes

Yield: Servings 4

INGREDIENTS:
- ¼ teaspoon freshly ground black pepper
- 1 tablespoon thinly cut fresh chives
- 1 teaspoon salt
- 2 cups shredded rotisserie chicken

- 2 leeks, white parts only, thinly cut
- 2 teaspoons grated or minced lemon zest
- 3 tablespoons unsalted butter
- 4 cups baby spinach
- 4 cups chicken broth

DIRECTIONS:

1. In a large pot, melt the butter on high heat.
2. Put in the leeks and sauté until tender and starting to brown, three to five minutes.
3. Put in the spinach, broth, salt, and pepper and bring to its boiling point.
4. Reduce the heat and cook till the spinach wilts, one to two minutes.
5. Place the chicken and cook until warmed through one to two minutes.
6. Drizzle with the chives and lemon zest before you serve.

NUTRITIONAL INFO: Calories: 256 ,Total Fat: 12g ,Total Carbohydrates: 9g ,Sugar: 3g ,Fiber: 2g ,Protein: 27g ,Sodium: 1483mg

LEMON CHICKEN SOUP

Time To Prepare: ten minutes

Time to Cook: 4 hours

Yield: Servings 4

INGREDIENTS:

- ¼ cup freshly squeezed lemon juice
- 1 yellow onion, chopped
- 2 boneless, skinless chicken breasts
- 2 cloves garlic, chopped
- 2 tablespoons chives, chopped
- 6 cups chicken broth
- Salt & pepper, to taste

DIRECTIONS:

1. Put in all the ingredients to a slow cooker and cook on high for 4 hours.
2. Once cooked, shred the chicken and stir back into the soup.

NUTRITIONAL INFO: Calories: 171 ,Carbohydrates: 6g ,Fiber: 1g Net ,Carbohydrates: 5g ,Fat: 6g ,Protein: 22g

CASHEW "HUMUS"

Time To Prepare: ten minutes

Time to Cook: 0 minutes

Yield: Servings 1

INGREDIENTS:

- ¼ Cup Water
- ¼ Teaspoon Sea Salt, Fine
- ½ Teaspoon Ground Ginger
- 1 Cup Cashews, Raw & Soaked in Water for fifteen Minutes & Drained
- 1 Tablespoon Olive Oil
- 1 Teaspoon Lemon juice, Fresh
- 2 Cloves Garlic
- 2 Teaspoon Coconut Aminos
- Pinch Cayenne Pepper

DIRECTIONS:

1. Blend all ingredients together, and ensure to scrape the sides.
2. Continue to combine until the desired smoothness is achieved, and then place in your fridge it before you serve.

NUTRITIONAL INFO: Calories: 112 ,Protein: 2.9 Grams ,Fat: 8.8 Grams ,Carbohydrates: 5.3 Grams

CASHEW CHEESE

Time To Prepare: 2 hours

Time to Cook: 0 minutes

Yield: Servings 6

INGREDIENTS:

- ¼ cup of fresh basil
- 1 cup of raw cashews
- 1 tablespoon of nutritional yeast
- Juice of ½ lemon
- Salt and pepper to taste

DIRECTIONS:

1. In a1 cup of water, soak the cashew for minimum 2 hours. Drain.
2. Put the cashews, lemon juice, nutritional yeast, and fresh basil into a food processor and pulse until the desired smoothness is achieved. Put in 1 tablespoon of water at a time to make it creamy, but not runny.
3. Flavor it with pepper and salt, then spread it on gluten-free bread or toast.
4. Store in an airtight jar in your fridge.

NUTRITIONAL INFO: ,Total Carbohydrates: 126g ,Fiber: 1g ,Net Carbohydrates: ,Protein: 4g ,Total Fat: 10g Calories: 126

MEDITERRANEAN STEW

Time To Prepare: ten minutes

Time to Cook: fifteen minutes

Yield: Servings 4

INGREDIENTS:
- 1 (19-ounce) can cannellini beans, drained and washed
- 1 (fifteen½-ounce) can chickpeas, drained and washed
- 1 cup Basic Vegetable Stock or low-sodium canned vegetable stock
- 1 teaspoon dried oregano
- 1 teaspoon red pepper, crushed or to taste
- 1½ cups artichoke hearts, quartered
- 2 cups roasted tomatoes
- 3 cloves garlic, crushed and minced
- 3 tablespoons olive oil
- 4 tablespoons grated Parmesan cheese
- Chopped Italian parsley, for decoration
- Chopped sun-dried tomatoes, for decoration
- Crumbled feta cheese, for decoration
- Fresh oregano leaves, for decoration
- Freshly ground black pepper, to taste
- Garlic-seasoned croutons, for decoration
- Salt, to taste

DIRECTIONS:
1. Warm the olive oil in a huge deep cooking pan on moderate heat and sauté the garlic for two to three minutes or until golden.
2. Lower the heat to moderate-low. Mix in the chickpeas, cannellini beans, roasted tomatoes, artichoke hearts, stock, Parmesan cheese, crushed red pepper, oregano, salt, and pepper. Cook and stir for approximately ten minutes. Serve in separate bowls, garnishing as you wish.

NUTRITIONAL INFO: Calories: 445 ,Fat: 16 g ,Protein: 18 g ,Sodium: 530 mg ,Fiber: 12 g ,Carbohydrates: 61 g

MINESTRONE SOUP WITH QUINOA

Time To Prepare: ten minutes

Time to Cook: twenty minutes

Yield: Servings 6

INGREDIENTS:
- ½ cup quinoa, washed well
- ½ red bell pepper, diced
- ½ teaspoon salt
- 1 (14 oz.) can cannellini beans, drained and washed well

- 1 (14 oz.) can diced tomatoes with its juice
- 1 bay leaf
- 1 cup packed kale, stemmed and meticulously washed
- 1 medium white onion, diced
- 1 small zucchini, diced
- 1 tablespoon freshly squeezed lemon juice
- 1 tablespoon ghee
- 2 carrots, chopped
- 2 celery stalks, diced
- 2 garlic cloves, minced
- 2 teaspoons dried rosemary
- 2 teaspoons dried thyme
- 5 cups vegetable broth
- Freshly ground black pepper

DIRECTIONS:

1. In a huge soup pot on moderate heat, put in the ghee, garlic, onion, carrots, and celery, and sauté for about three minutes.
2. Put in the zucchini and red bell pepper, and sauté for a couple of minutes.
3. Mix in the broth, tomatoes, beans, kale, quinoa, lemon juice, rosemary, thyme, bay leaf, and salt, and flavor with black pepper. Put it to a simmer, reduce the heat temperature, cover, and cook for fifteen minutes, or until the quinoa is cooked. Take away the bay leaf and discard it. Serve hot.

NUTRITIONAL INFO: Calories: 319 ,Total Fat: 5g ,Saturated Fat: 2g ,Cholesterol: 0mg ,Carbohydrates: 42g ,Fiber: 9g ,Protein: 18g

MOONG DAAL

Time To Prepare: fifteen minutes

Time to Cook: thirty minutes

Yield: Servings 6

INGREDIENTS:

- ½ Cup Tomatoes (Diced)
- ½ Dried Red Chili Pepper
- ½ Teaspoon Ginger Root (Grated)
- ½ Teaspoon Ground Turmeric
- 1 Pinch Asafoetida
- 1 Teaspoon Cumin Seed
- 1 Teaspoon Jalapeno (Diced)
- 1/4 Cup Cilantro (Chopped)
- 2 Cloves Garlic (Chopped)
- 2 Teaspoons Vegetable Oil

- 2½ Cups Moong Dal (Rinsed)
- 2½ Cups Water
- 3 Teaspoons Lemon Juice
- Salt

DIRECTIONS:
1. Soak daal for thirty minutes before boiling in water with salt until thick.
2. Put in ginger, jalapeno, tomato, lemon juice, and turmeric.
3. Heat cumin seed and red Chile pepper in a pan before you put in asafoetida powder and garlic.
4. Combine with split peas and serve with cilantro.

NUTRITIONAL INFO: Calories: 330 kcal ,Carbohydrates: 57 g ,Fat: 3 g ,Protein: 21 g

MUSHROOM AND THYME SOUP

Time To Prepare: five minutes

Time to Cook: twenty minutes

Yield: Servings 4

INGREDIENTS:
- ¼ cup butter
- 12 ounces (340 g) wild mushrooms, chopped
- 2 garlic cloves, minced
- 2 teaspoons thyme leaves
- 4 cups vegetable broth
- 5 ounces (142 g) crème fraiche
- From the cupboard:
- Salt and freshly ground black pepper, to taste

DIRECTIONS:
1. Place the butter in a deep cooking pan and melt on moderate heat.
2. Put in the minced garlic and cook for a minutes or until aromatic.
3. Put in the chopped mushrooms, and drizzle with salt and black pepper. Stir to blend and cook for about ten minutes or until the mushrooms are soft.
4. Put in the vegetable broth and bring the soup to its boiling point. Stir continuously. Reduce the heat and simmer the soup for about ten minutes or until it becomes slightly thick.
5. Pour the soup in a blender, and pulse until smooth, then fold in the crème fraiche.
6. Move the soup in a big container and top with thyme leaves before you serve.

NUTRITIONAL INFO: calories: 282 ,total fat: 25.1g ,net carbs: 6.3g ,protein: 7.8g